3 Workbook

Pippa and Pop

American English

Colin Sage
with Caroline Nixon & Michael Tomlinson

CAMBRIDGE UNIVERSITY PRESS

Map of the book

	VOCABULARY	LANGUAGE	SOUNDS AND LETTERS	LITERACY AND VALUES	NUMBERS	CROSS-CURRICULAR
Introduction Page 4						
1 **Me!** Page 6	Review Level 2: characters, numbers, likes *angry, bored, excited, scared, sleepy, surprised*	*Hello! What's your name? I'm (Kim).* *How old are you? I'm (eight).* *I like (books).* *What's her / his name?* *She's (Kim). He's (Dan).* *How old is she / he?* *She's / He's (eight).* *He's / She's / I'm (bored).* *He isn't / She isn't / I'm not (bored).*	Review Level 2 letter sounds: *b, m, t, g, p, d, k, n, s, h*	*Jane's name* Be yourself	Review numbers: *1 – 20*	Music: Emotions from music
2 **My day** Page 18	*brush my hair, brush my teeth, get dressed, have breakfast, wake up, wash my face* *go to bed, have dinner, have a snack, listen to a story, play with friends, take a bath*	*I (wake up) (in the morning / every day).* *They / We (play with friends) (after school / in the evening).* *We / They don't (take a bath).*	Letter sound /ʃ/ *(sh)*	*Brush your hair, Leo!* Take care of yourself	Adding by counting	Social studies: Times of day
3 **My home** Page 30	*make the bed, pick up the toys, set the table, sweep the floor, wash the clothes, wash the dishes* *bed, bookcase, cabinet, lamp, rug, toy box*	*He / She (washes the dishes).* *I (sweep the floor).* *It's (under / in / on / next to) the (bed).*	Letter sound / **k** / *(ck)*	*Goldilocks and the three bears* Respect other people's things	Numbers: *10, 20, 30, 40*	Social studies: Objects at home
Units 1–3 Review Page 42–43						
4 **My sports** Page 44	*badminton, baseball, basketball, field hockey, soccer, tennis* *bouncing, catching, hitting, kicking, rolling, throwing*	*They're / She's / He's playing (soccer).* *She's / He's / They're / I'm (throwing) the ball.*	Letter sound / **ŋ** / *(ng)*	*A sport for Grace* Persevere	Subtracting by counting	Physical education: Team sports

	VOCABULARY	LANGUAGE	SOUNDS AND LETTERS	LITERACY AND VALUES	NUMBERS	CROSS-CURRICULAR
5 **My free time** Page 56	*cooking dinner, drawing pictures, listening to music, playing video games, reading books, watching TV* *go roller skating, go swimming, play a board game, play with building blocks, play hide-and-seek, play outside*	*I / We like (reading books).* *Let's (go swimming / play a board game)!* *Can I (come / play)?*	Letter sounds / ʊ / (short *oo*) and / uː / (long *oo*)	*Jack loves reading* Join in and help	Numbers: *50, 60*	Art: Paintings, photographs, and sculptures
6 **My food** Page 68	*cake, candy, chips, chocolate, grapes, pineapple* *beans, cereal, fruit, meat, rice, vegetables*	*Would you like some (chocolate)?* *Yes, please. / No, thank you.* *I'd like some (candy), please.* *I / We have (meat and rice) for (breakfast / lunch / dinner).*	Letter sound / tʃ / *(ch)*	*Share, Ricky Raccoon!* Share	Estimating quantity	Science: Salty, sour, and sweet
Units 4–6 Review Page 80–81						
7 **Animals** Page 82	*crocodile, elephant, hippo, monkey, snake, tiger* *duck, giraffe, lizard, parrot, spider, zebra*	*There's (a monkey).* *There are (three) (monkeys).* *There are (lots of) (snakes).* *They're (giraffes). They have (long necks / long legs / stripes / short legs / big feet / long tails / sharp teeth).* *They're (fast).*	Letter sound / θ / *(th)*	*The mouse and the lion* Be friendly	Numbers: *70, 80*	Science: Where animals live
8 **Plants** Page 94	*garden, plants, rain, seeds, soil, sun* *beautiful, clean, dirty, new, old, ugly*	*What do plants need?* *Plants need (sun / rain / soil).* *What (beautiful) (flowers)!* *What (a dirty) (nose)!*	Letter sound / iː / *(ee, ea)*	*Sophia's garden* Work together	Measuring length	Science: How plants grow
9 **My town** Page 106	*hospital, playground, restaurant, school, store, supermarket* *doctor, farmer, nurse, sales clerk, teacher, waiter*	*Where are you / we going?* *I'm / We're going to the (supermarket).* *A (teacher) works in a (school).* *He / She works on a farm.* *Where does (a teacher) work?* *Does (a nurse) work (in) a (hospital)?* *Yes, he / she does. No, he / she doesn't.*	Letter sound / eɪ / *(ay, ai)*	*Big-city cat and small-town cat* Appreciate what you have	Numbers: *90, 100*	Social studies: Jobs
Units 7–9 Review Page 118–119						

Hello again!

Look. Find. Circle.

Look. Match. Say.

1 Me!

Listen again. Look. Stick. Point.

Look. Count. Match. Say.

At home Ask a friend *What's your name? How old are you?*

Look. Find. Circle. Say.

3 6 7 8

3 5 6 7

5 6 7 8

3 5 6 8

3 5 7 8

1 **Language practice:** *What's your / her / his name? I'm / She's / He's (Pippa / Dan / Kim / Tinks / Pop). How old are you / is she / is he? I'm / He's / She's (six / five / eight / three).*

6 Listen again. Look. Circle. Say.

b s

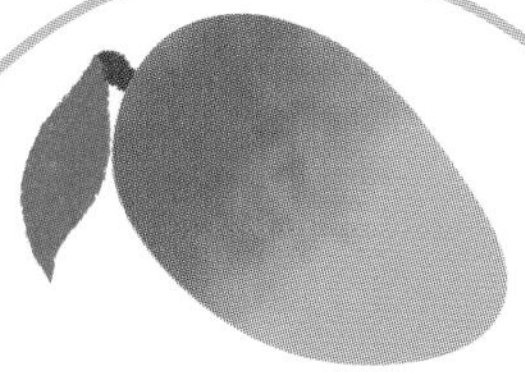

m p

n t

g b

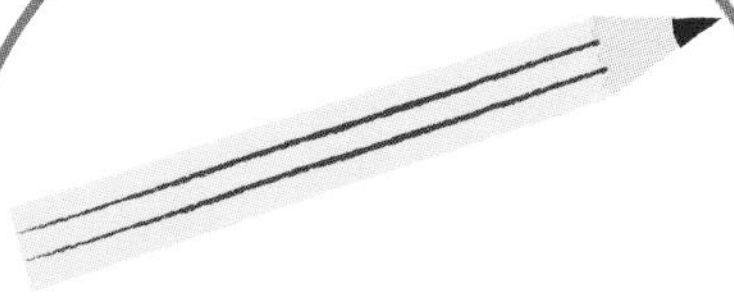

h p

d m

t k

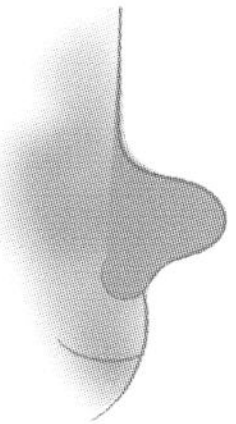

n g

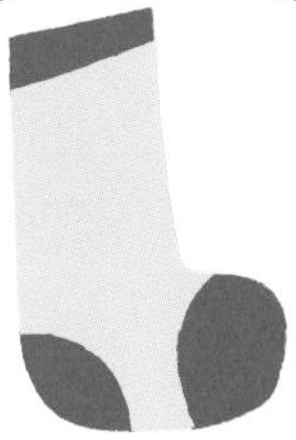

s d

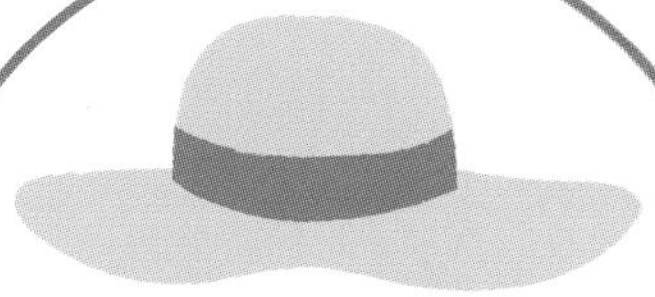

k h

Look. Point. Circle.

Look. Find. Draw.

At home

What do you like about yourself?

Look. Find. Circle. Say.

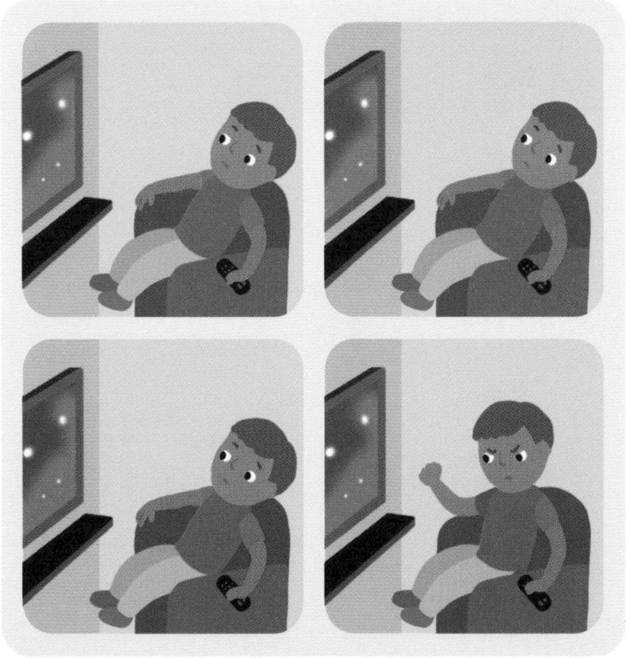

Look. Find. Match. Say.

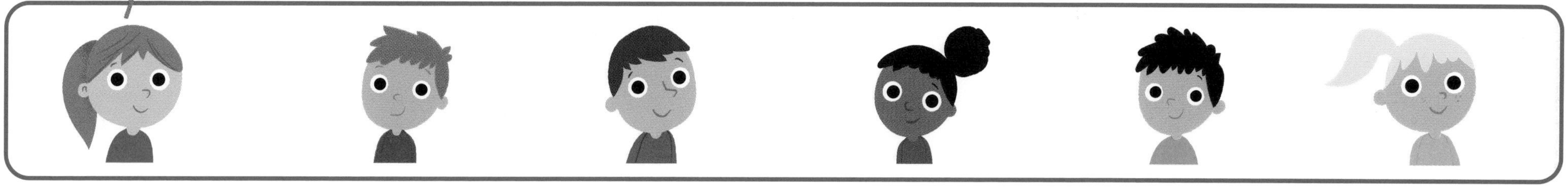

Look. Draw. Count. Say.

1
2
3
4
5
6
7
8
9
10

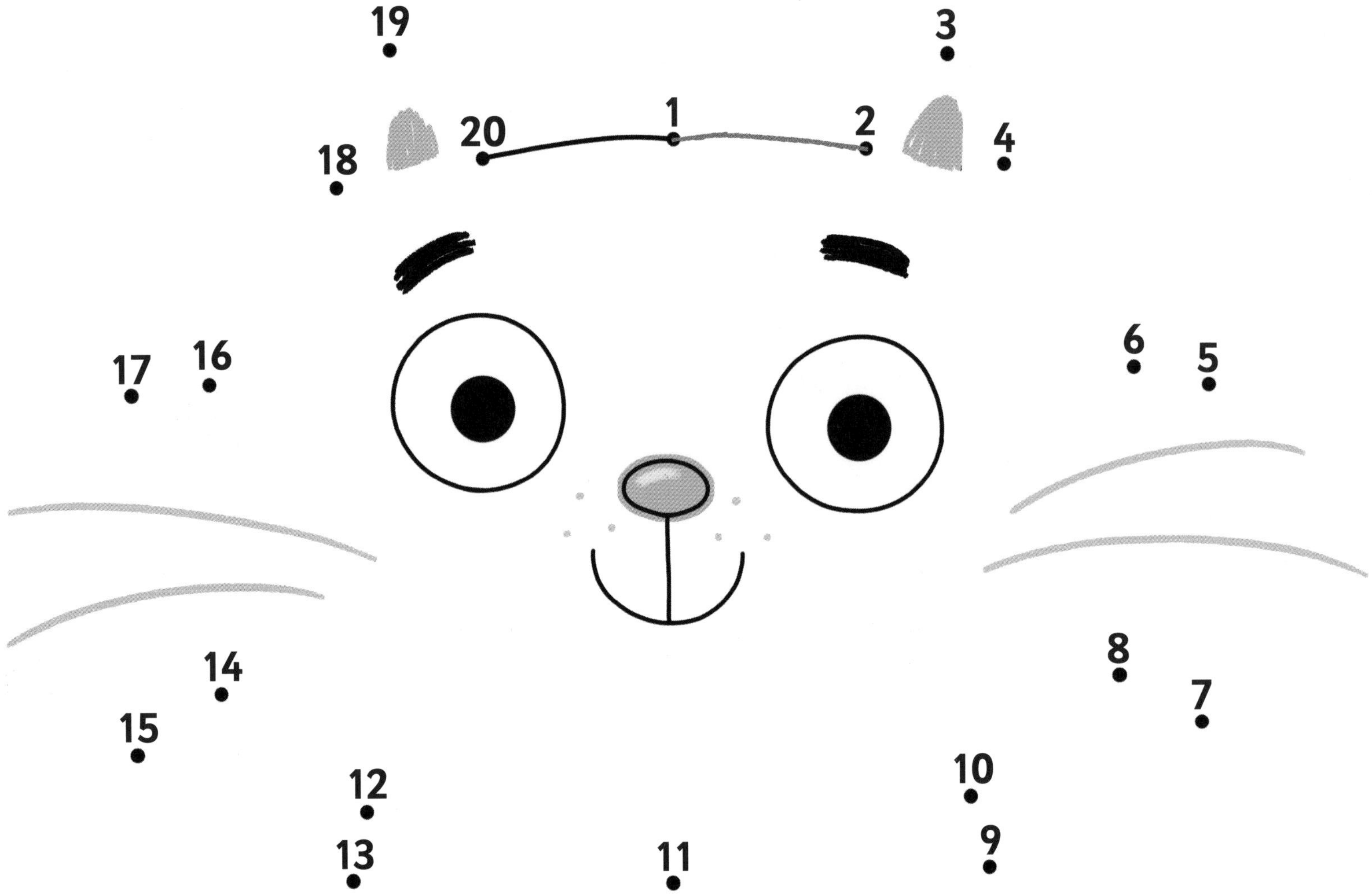

11
12
13
14
15
16
17
18
19
20

10 Listen again. Draw.

At home Listen to some music together.
Say how it makes you feel.

Look. Draw. Say.

1 *I'm / She's / He's (surprised). I'm not / He isn't / She isn't (bored).*

Point. Say. Draw.

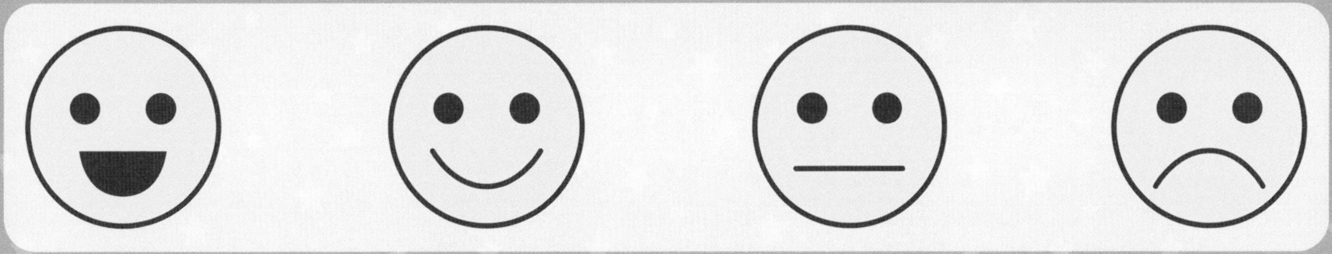

He's Pop. He's five.

2 My day

12 **Listen again.** **Look.** **Stick.** **Point.**

Look. Match. Say.

Look. Find. Circle. Say.

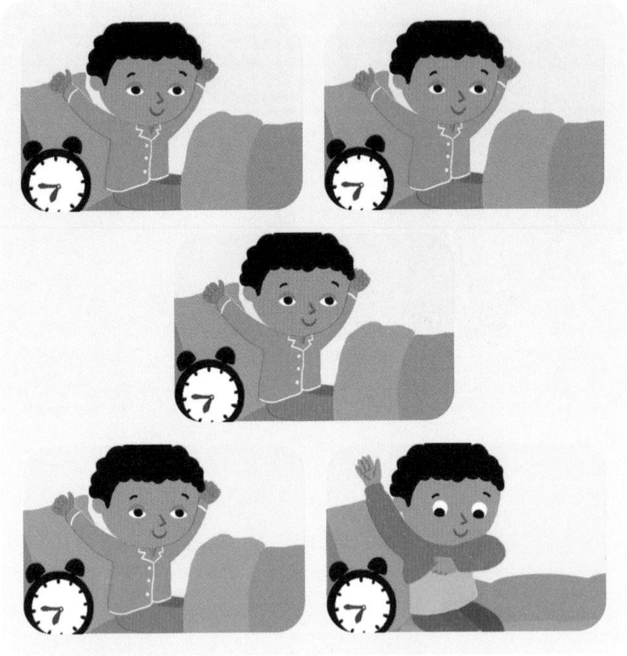

2 **Language practice:** *I (wash my face / brush my teeth / wake up / get dressed / brush my hair / have breakfast) (in the morning / every day).*

15 **Listen again. Color. Trace. Say.**

sh

Look. Point. Circle.

Look. Trace.

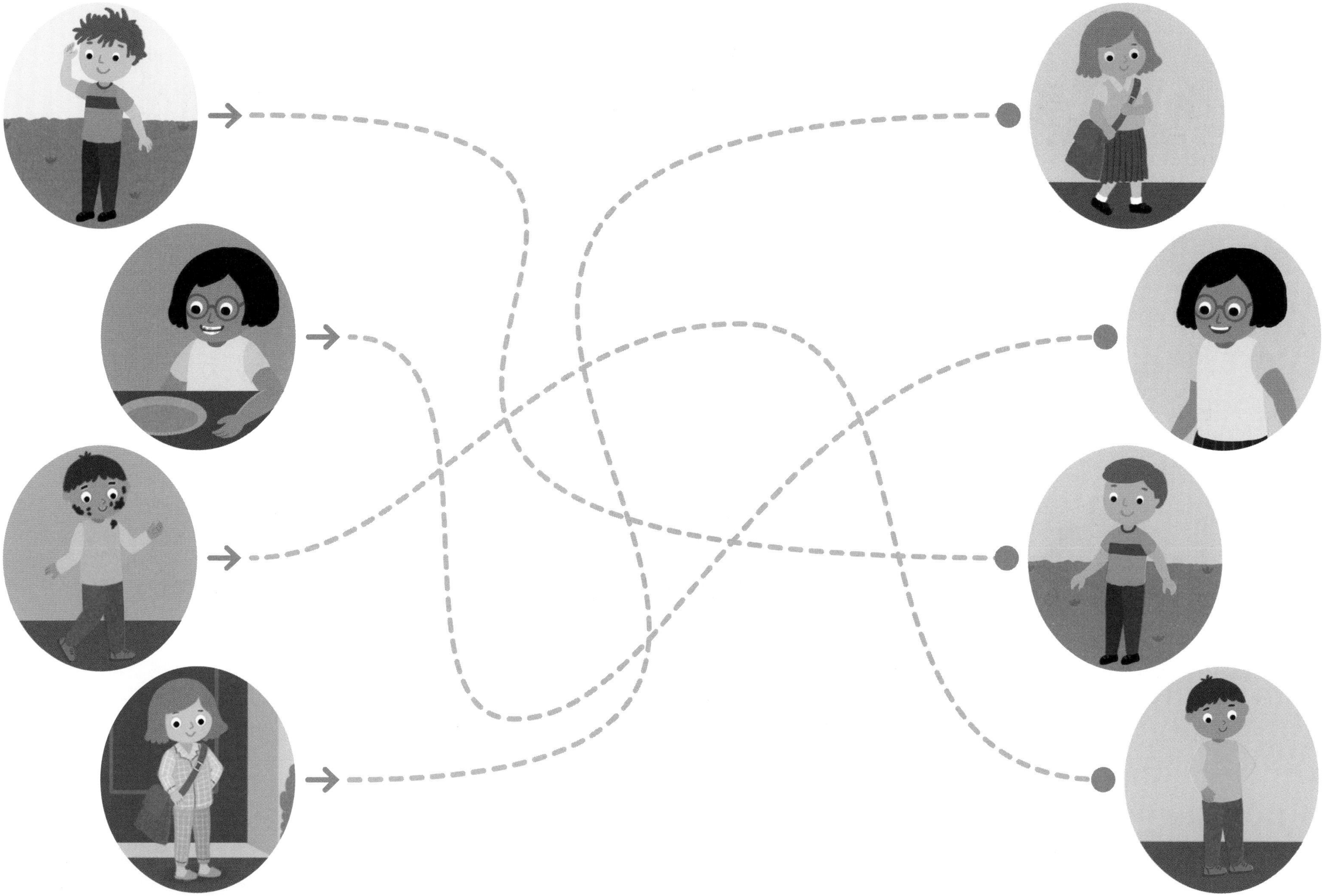

At home How do you take care of yourself?

Look. Find. Circle. Say.

2 **Vocabulary practice:** *play with friends, have a snack, take a bath, listen to a story, go to bed, have dinner*

Look. Find. Circle. Say.

Language practice: *They / We (listen to a story / play with friends / have a snack / go to bed / take a bath / have dinner) (after school / in the evening). We / They don't (take a bath).*

Look. Count. Match. Say.

8 + 1 =	7
4 + 4 =	8
6 + 4 =	9
5 + 2 =	10

At home Make a new adding question.

Look. Circle. Say.

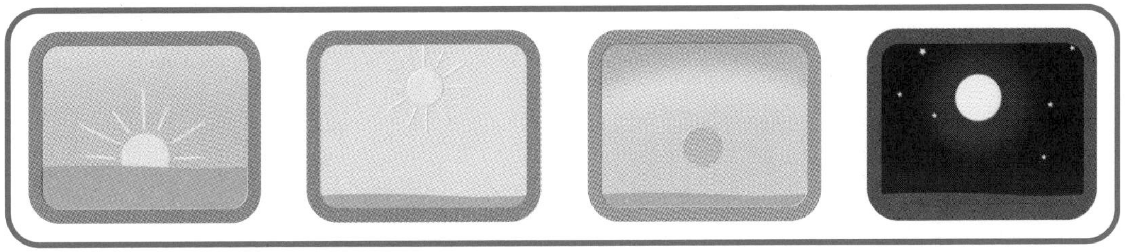

Look. Draw. Say.

2 *I (listen to a story) (every day / in the morning / in the evening).*

Point. Say. Draw.

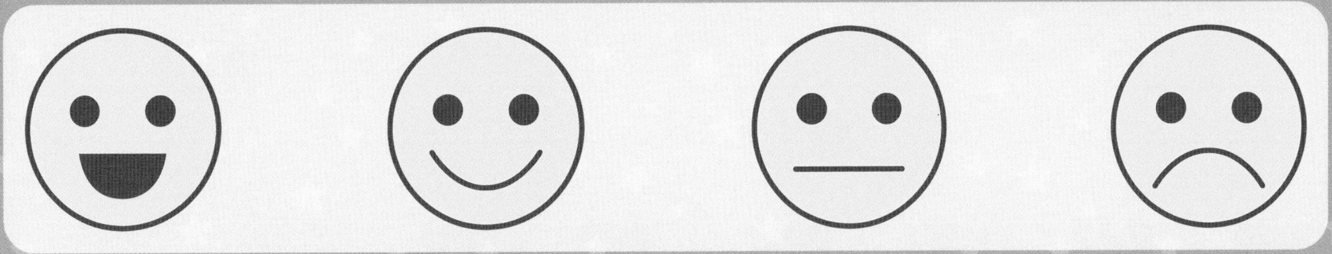

I / We / They (wake up / have dinner / listen to a story / have breakfast / play with friends) in the (morning / evening). I / We / They don't (take a bath) (every day / after school).

3 My home

20 Listen again. Look. Stick. Point.

Look. Find. Circle. Say.

At home What do you do at home?

Look. Match. Say.

3 **Language practice:** *He / She (sets the table / sweeps the floor / picks up the toys / washes the dishes / makes the bed). I (wash the clothes).*

23 Listen again. Color. Trace. Say.

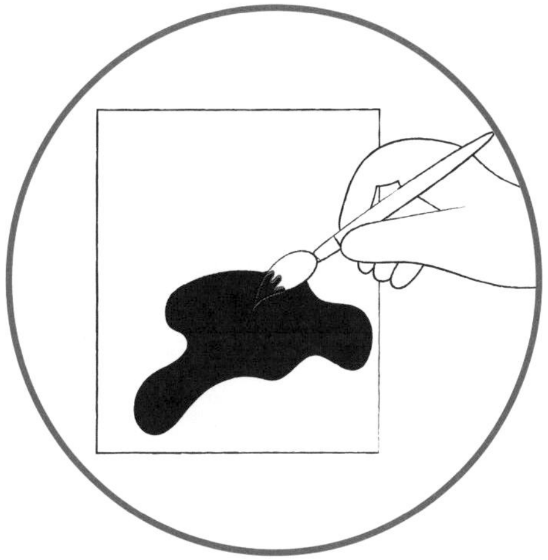

ck

Look. Point. Circle.

Look. Find. Color.

At home

How do you respect other people's things?

Look. Match. Say.

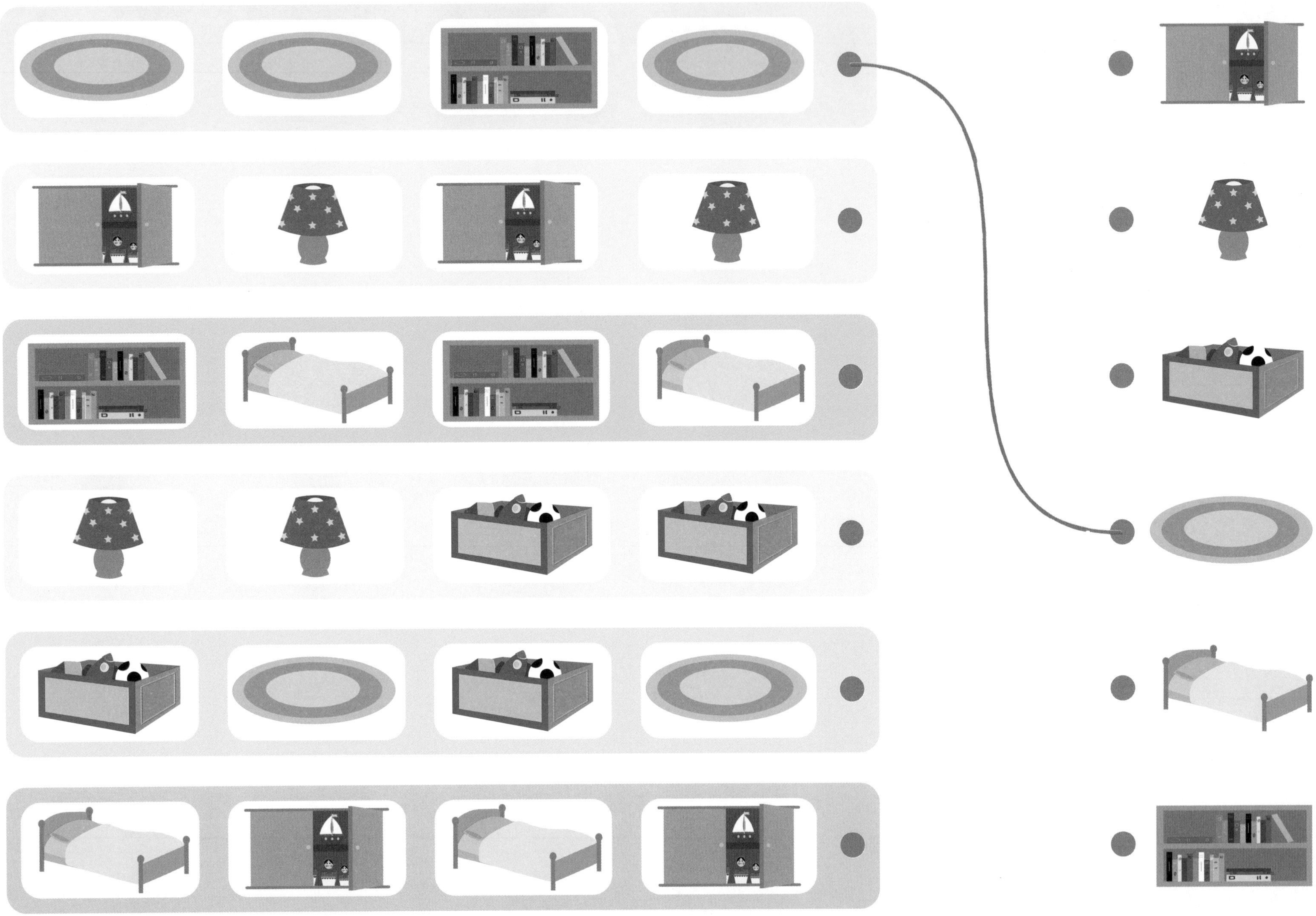

Look. Find. Circle. Say.

At home

Look in your bedroom. How many sentences can you make?

Numbers

Look. Count. Circle. Say.

10

20

30

40

20

30

30

40

Look. Color. Say.

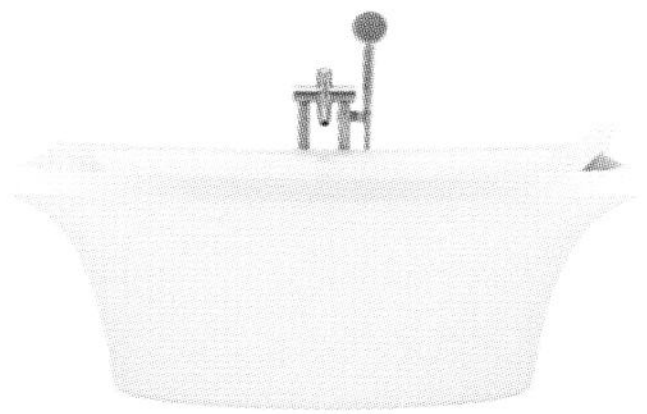

Look. Draw. Say.

3 *He / She (washes the dishes). I (sweep the floor) (in the morning).*

Point. Say. Draw.

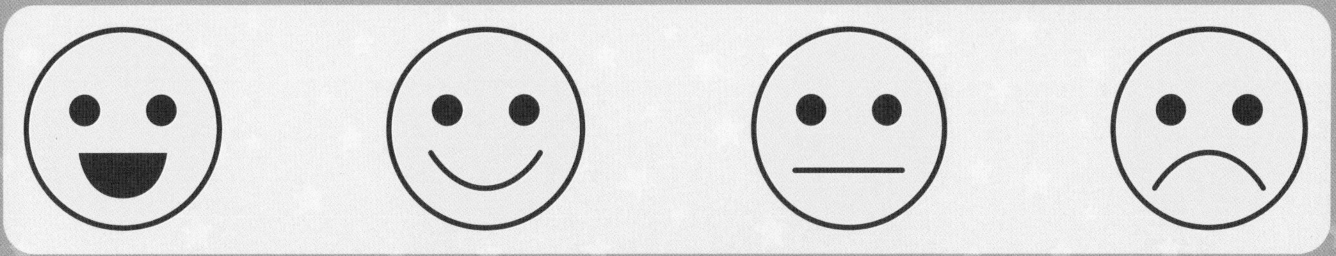

Look. Find. Match. Say.

Count. Match. Trace. Say.

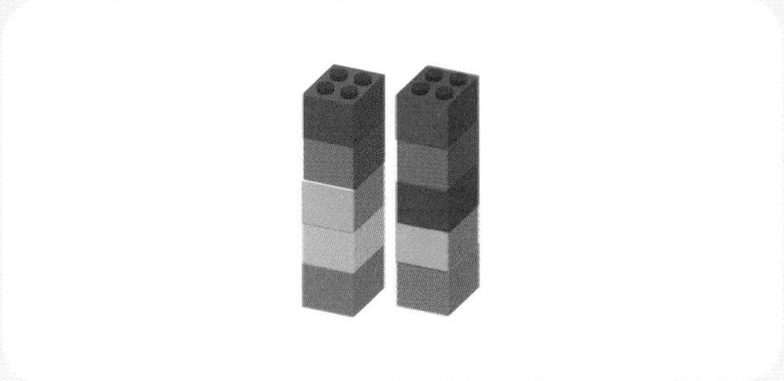

10

20

30

40

4 My sports

30 Listen again. Look. Stick. Point.

Look. Match. Say.

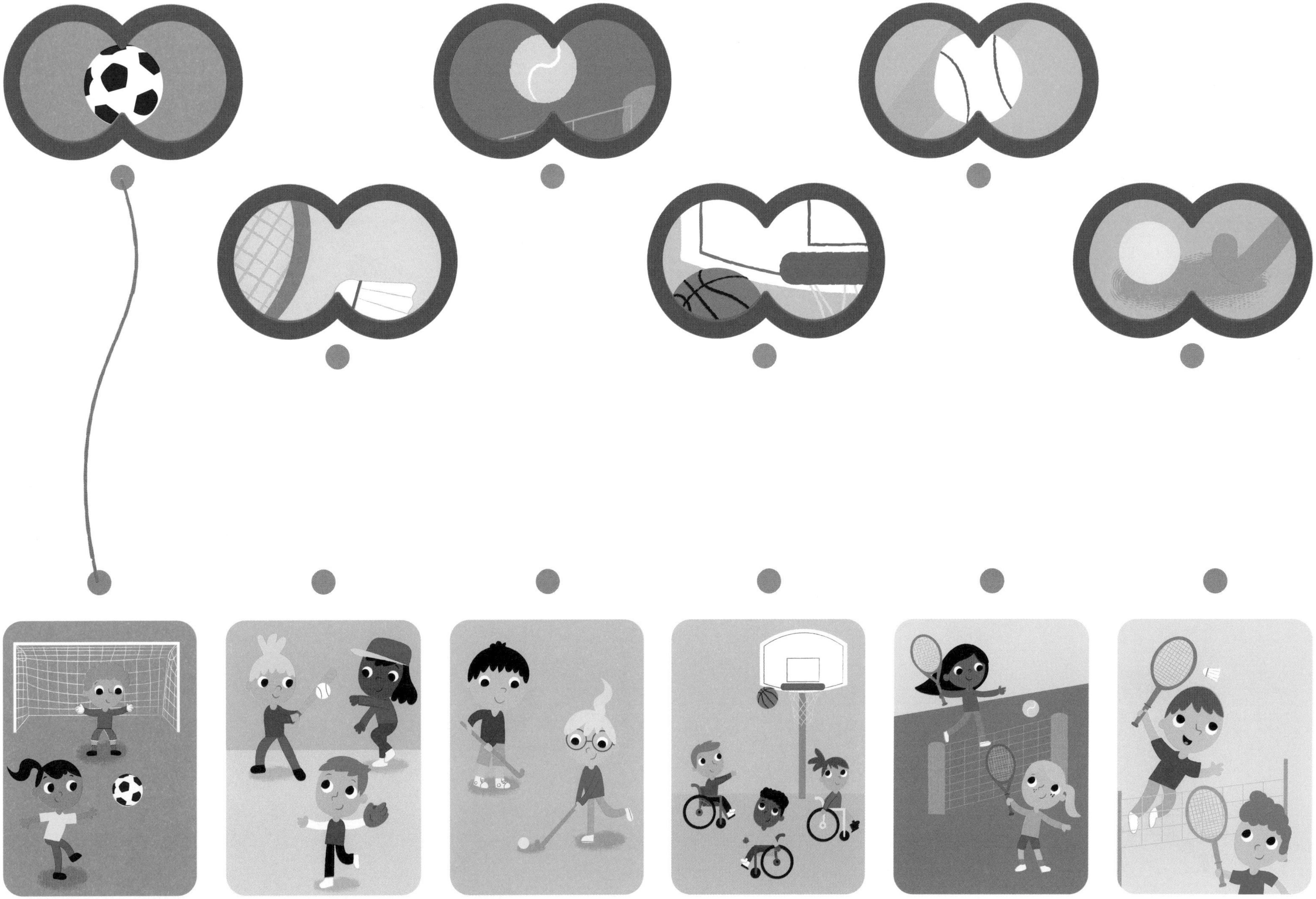

At home Which sports do you like?

Look. Find. Circle. Say.

4 **Language practice:** *She's / He's / They're playing (tennis / soccer / basketball / baseball / badminton / field hockey).*

33 **Listen again. Find. Circle. Trace. Say.**

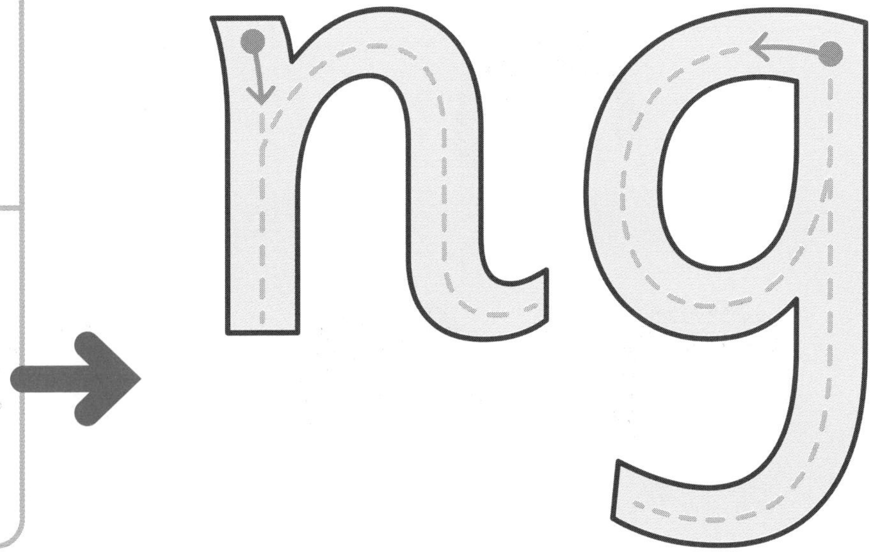

Look. Point. Circle.

Look. Trace.

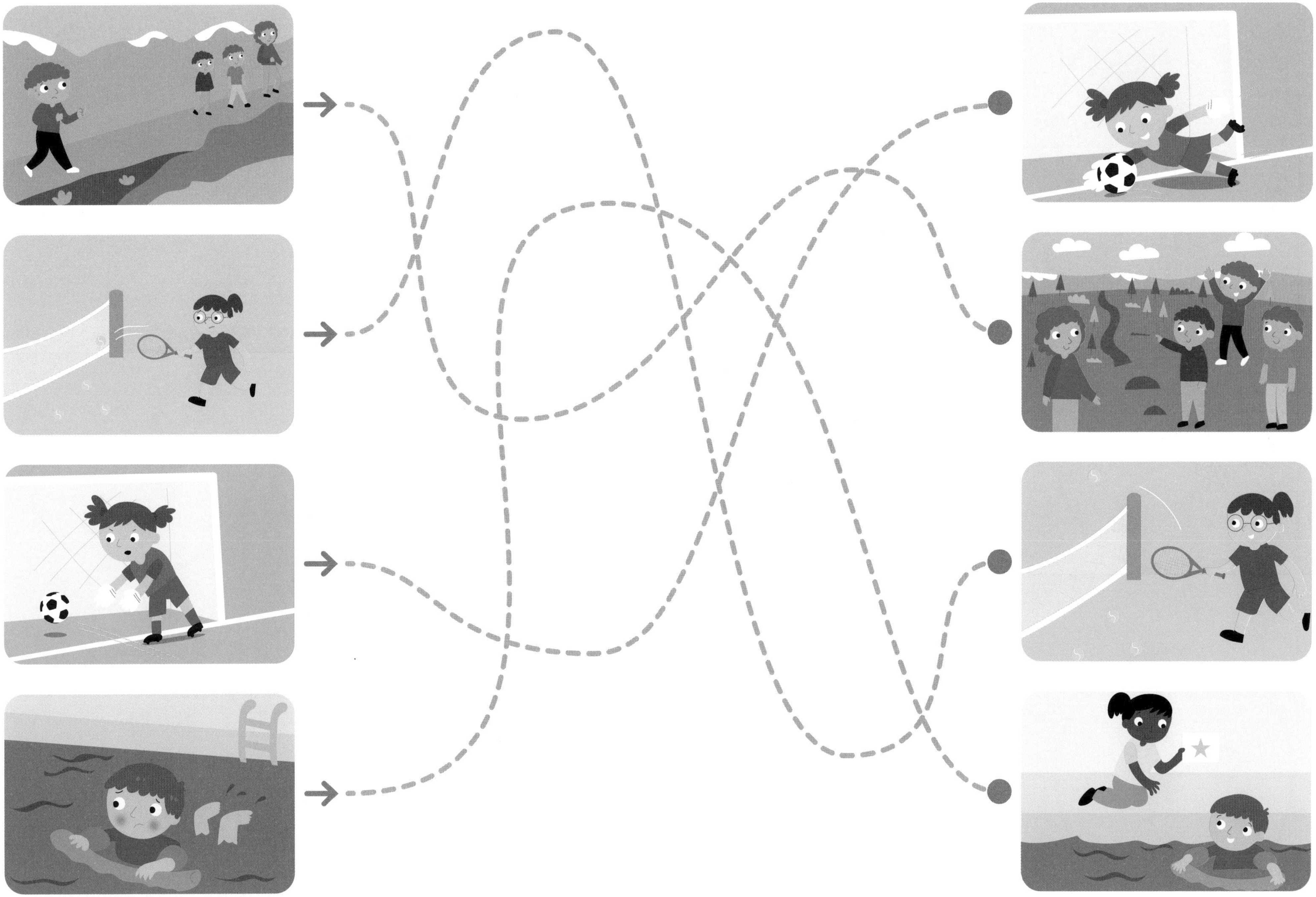

At home When do you persevere?

Look. Match. Say.

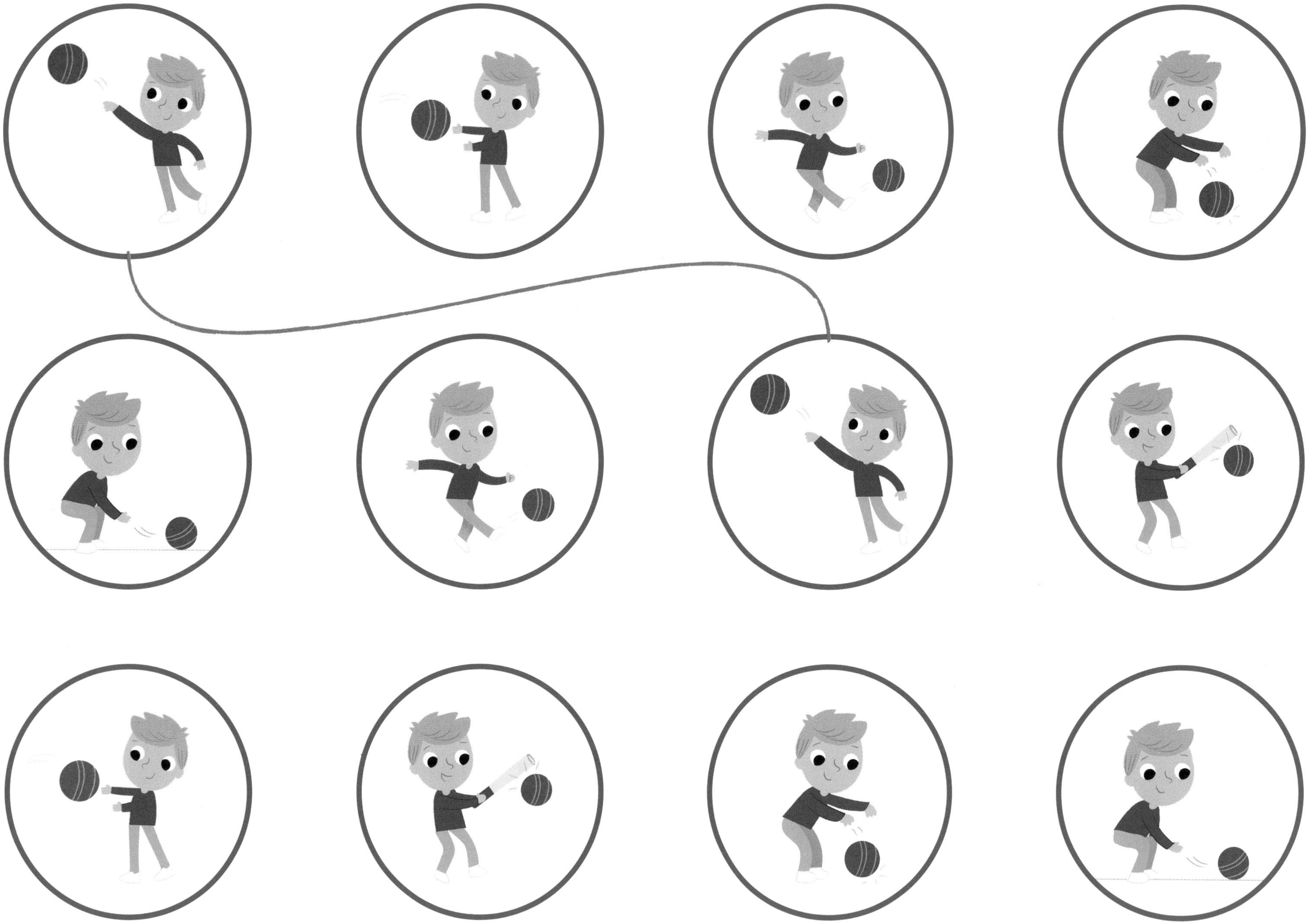

4 **Vocabulary practice:** *throwing, catching, kicking, bouncing, rolling, hitting*

Look. Draw. Say.

Look. Count. Match. Say.

7 − 4 =

5 − 3 =

10 − 5 =

6 − 2 =

2

3

4

5

At home Make a new subtracting question.

Look. Find. Circle.

Look. Draw. Say.

4 *She's / He's / They're (throwing / catching) the ball.*

Point. Say. Draw.

5 My free time

39 Listen again. Look. Stick. Point.

Look. Find. Circle. Say.

Look. Match. Say.

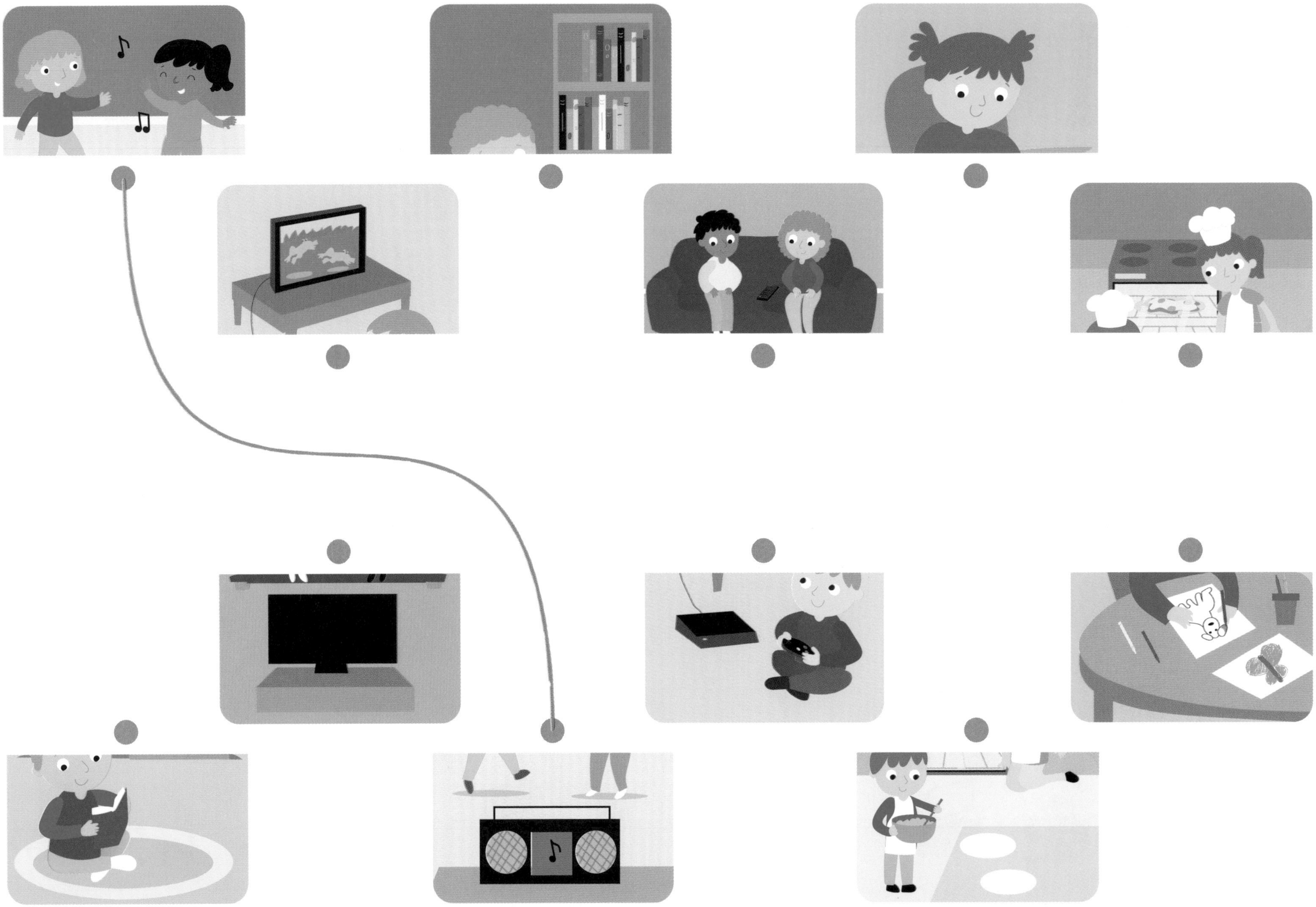

5 **Language practice:** *I / We like (listening to music / playing video games / reading books / watching TV / drawing pictures / cooking).*

42 Listen again. Find. Circle. Trace. Say.

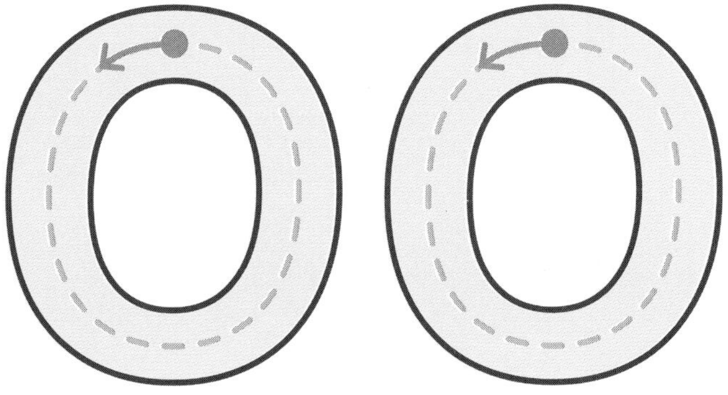

43 Listen again. Look. 123 Number.

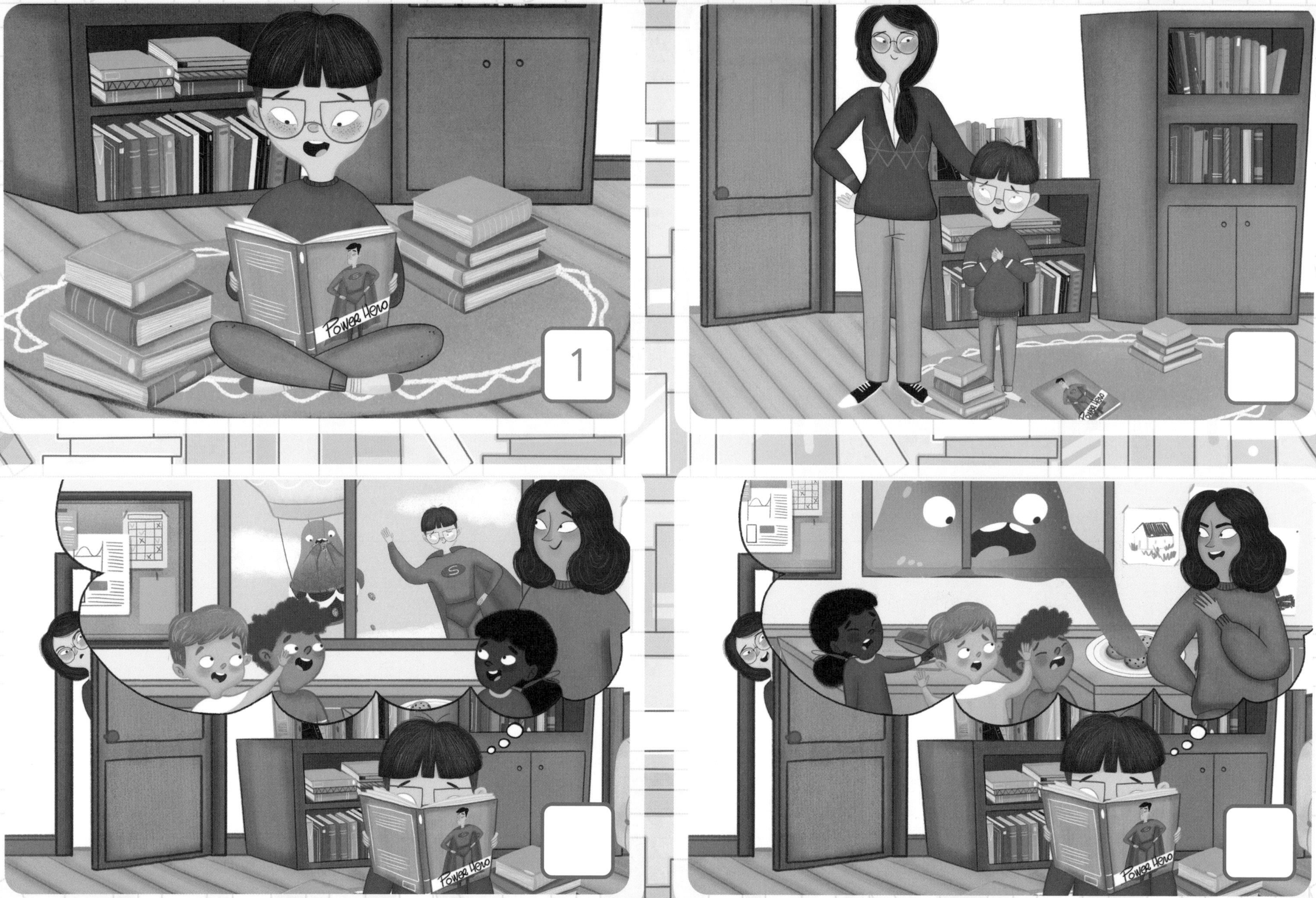

Look. Find. Draw.

At home

When do you join in and help?

Look. Find. Circle. Say.

5 **Vocabulary practice:** *play outside, go roller skating, play a board game, play with building blocks, go swimming, play hide-and-seek*

Look. Match. Say.

Language practice: *Let's (play hide-and-seek / go swimming / go roller skating / play with building blocks / play outside / play a board game)! Can I (play / come)?*

Look. Count. Circle. Say.

10

20

30

40

50

60

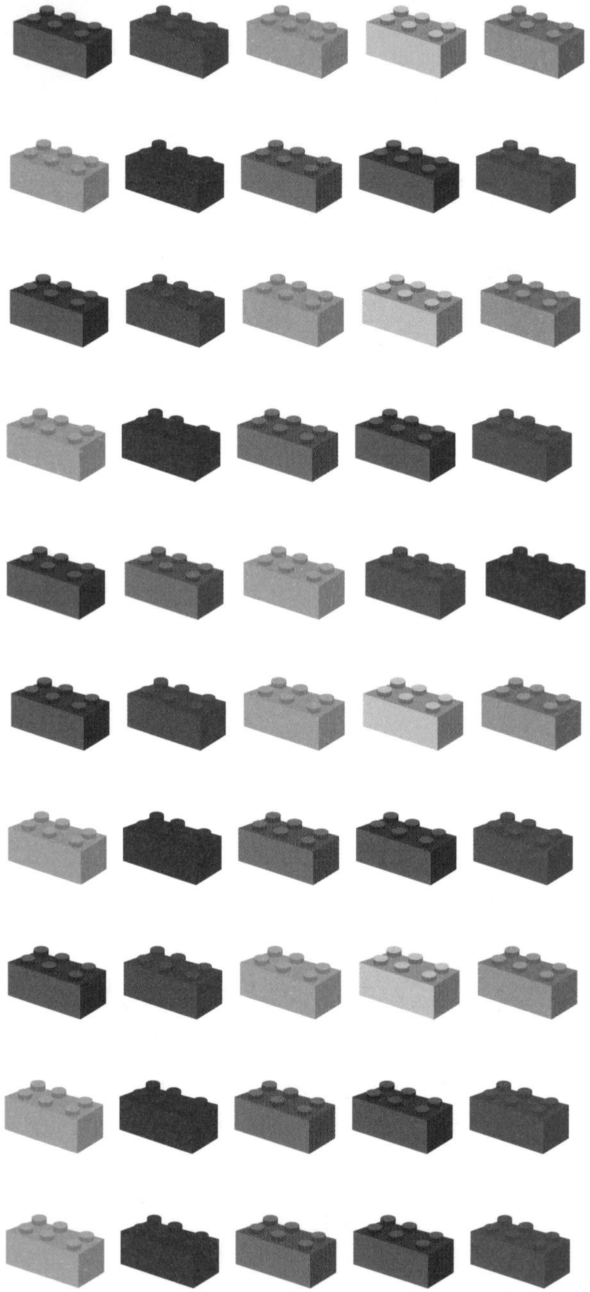

10

20

30

40

50

60

Look. Circle. Say.

Look. Draw. Say.

5 *I / We like (reading books).*

Point. Say. Draw.

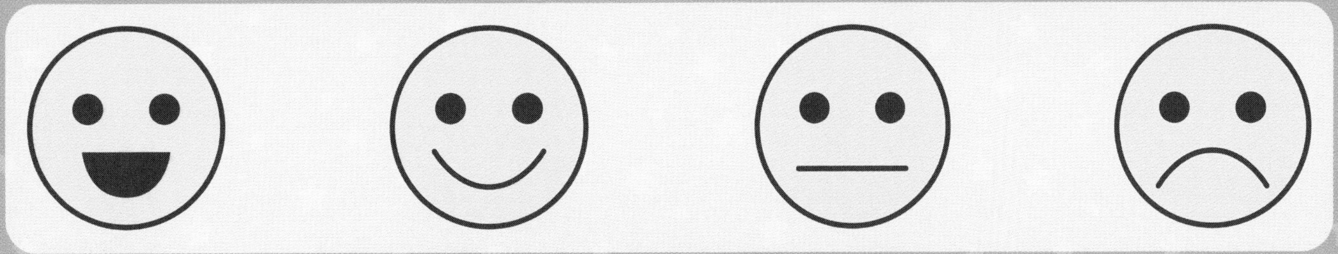

6 My food

Listen again. Look. Stick. Point.

Look. Match. Say.

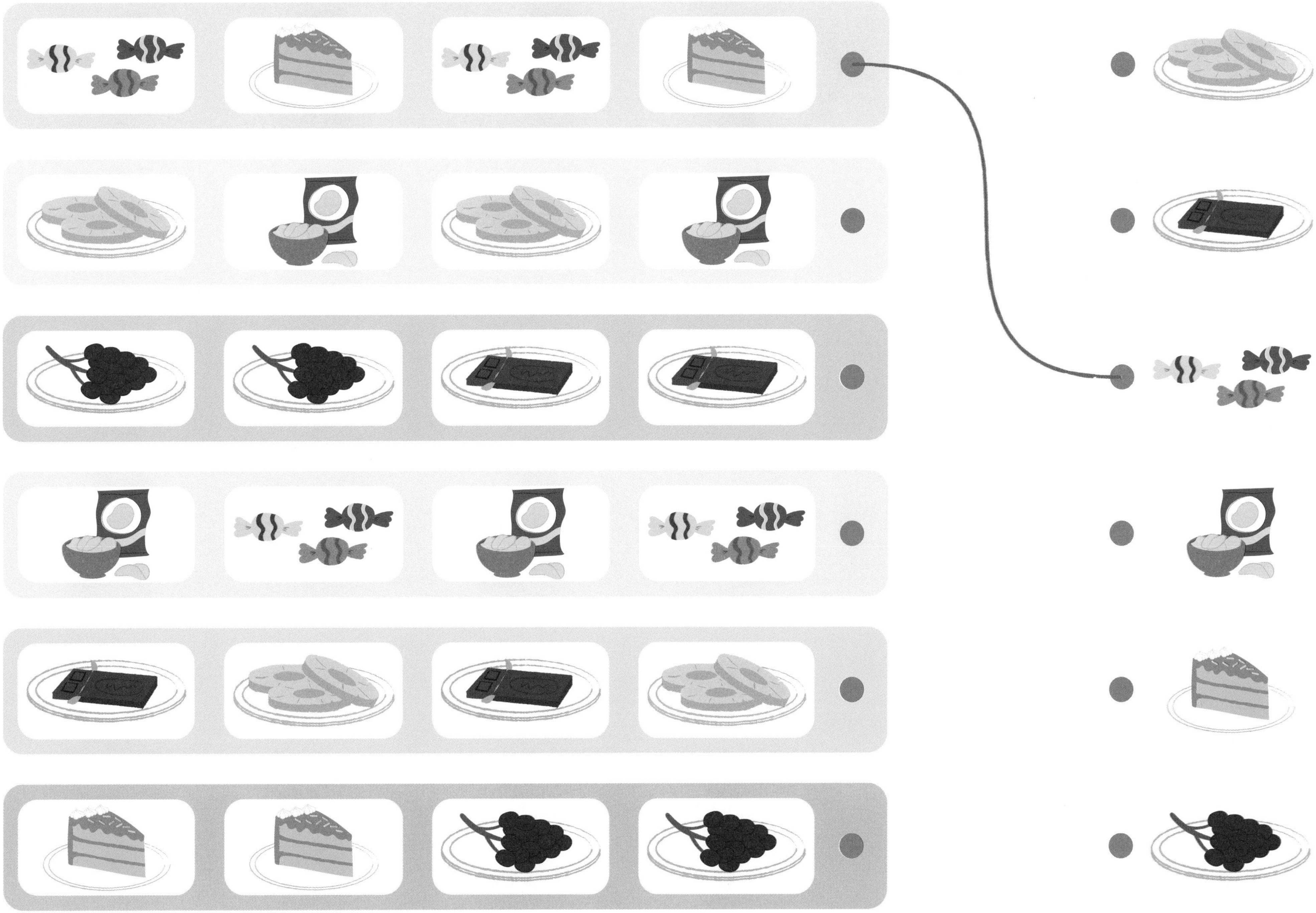

Look. Trace. Say.

6 **Language practice:** *Would you like some (candy / pineapple / grapes / chocolate / cake / chips)? Yes, please. / No, thank you.*

51 Listen again. Find. Circle. Trace. Say.

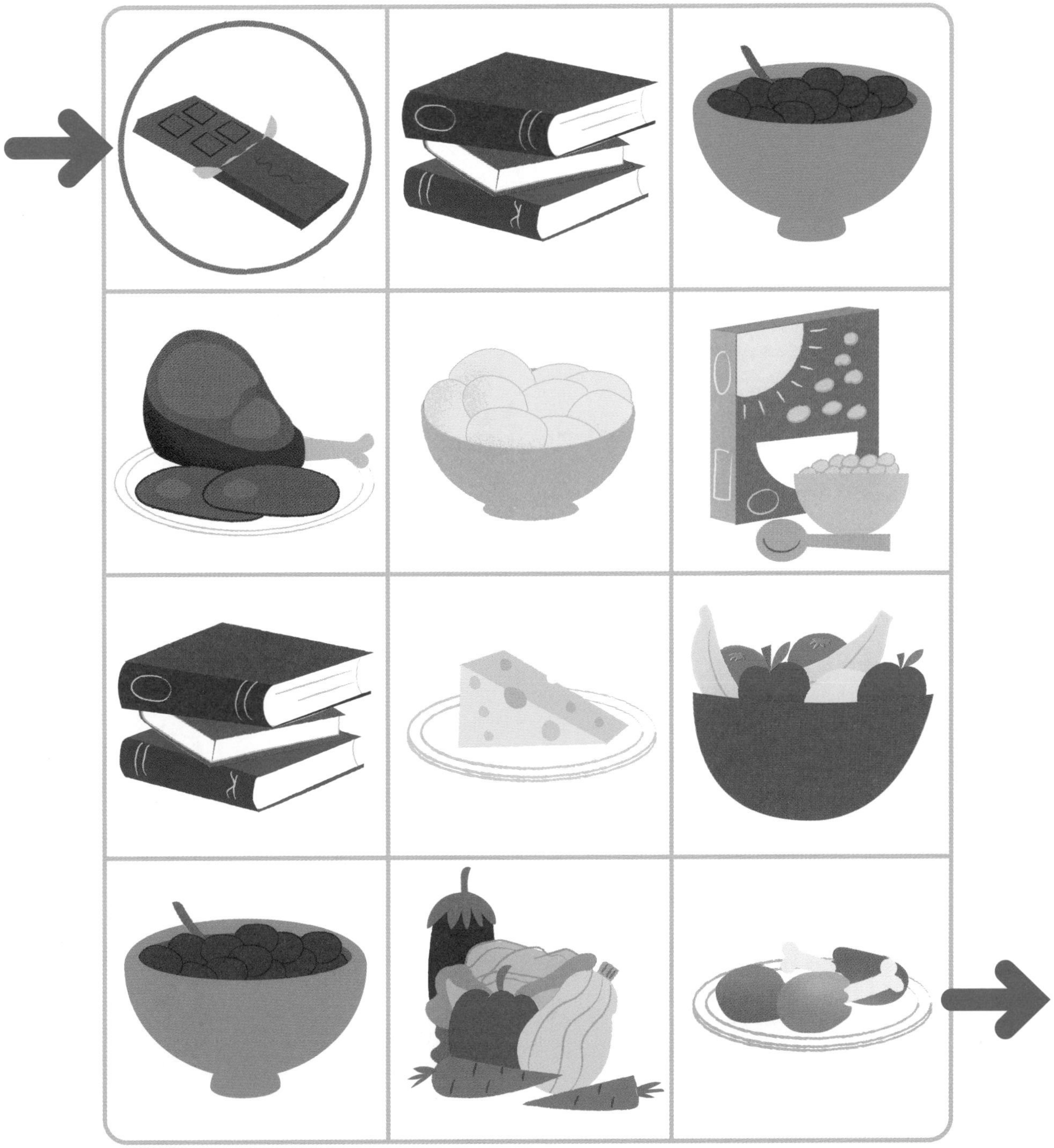

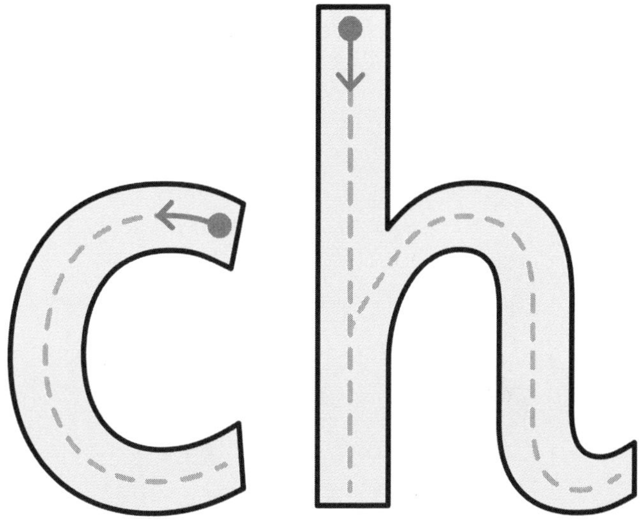

Look. Point. Circle.

Look. Find. Color.

At home

When do you share?

Look. Match. Say.

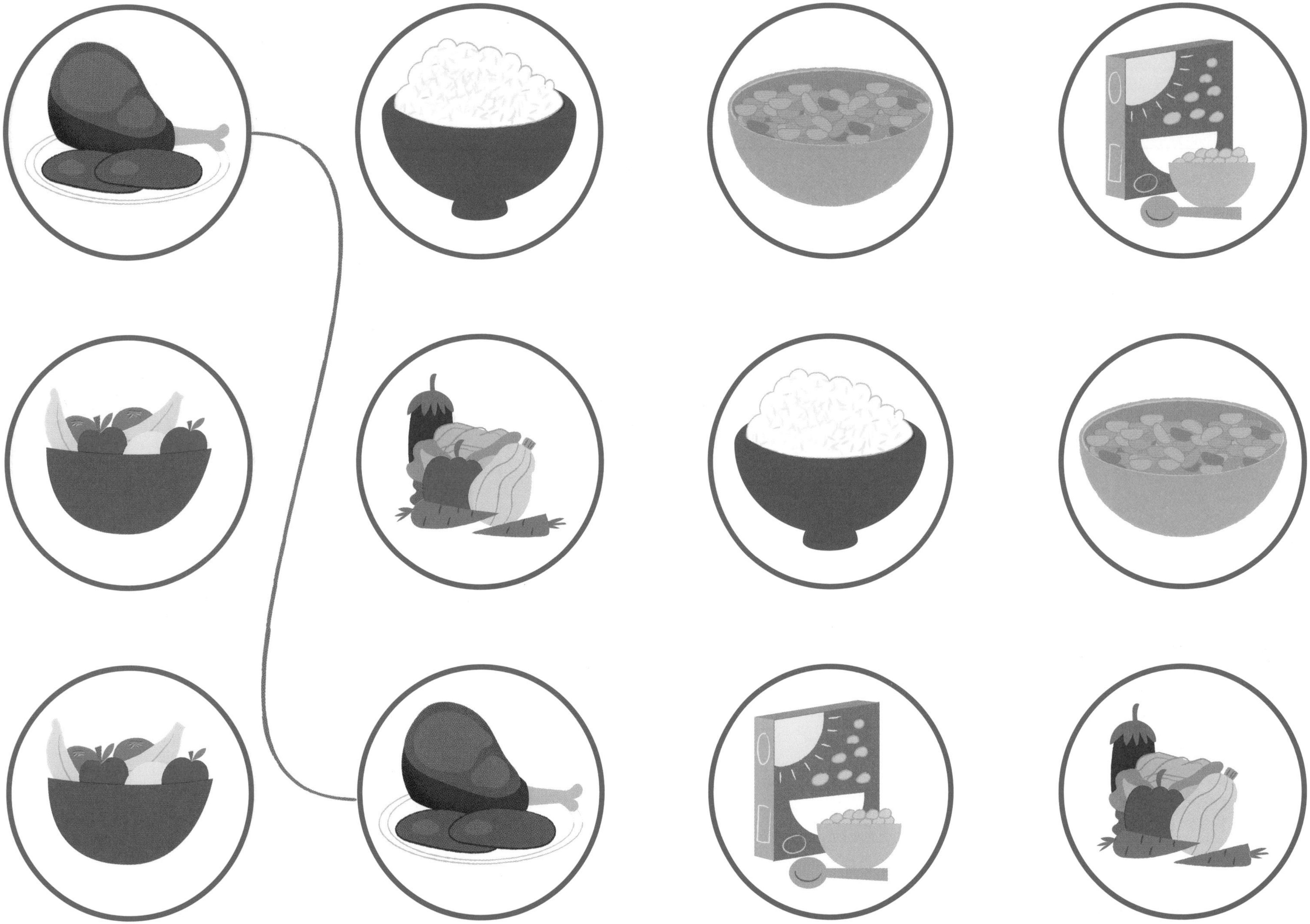

Look. Match. Say.

Look. Write. Count. Match.

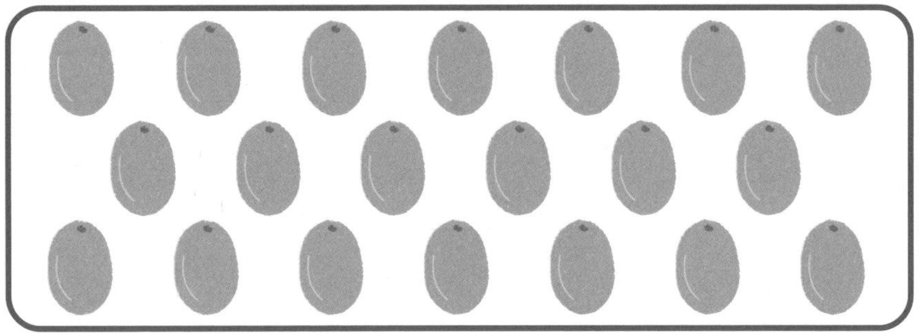

______

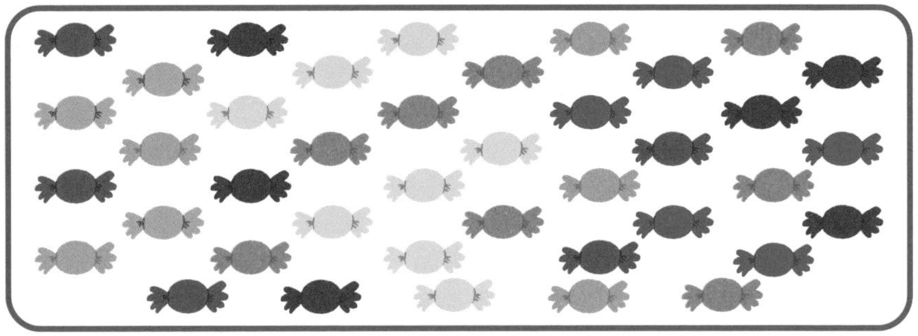

______

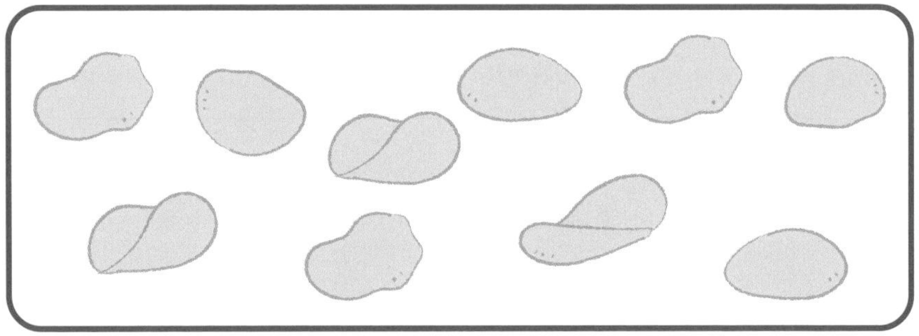

______

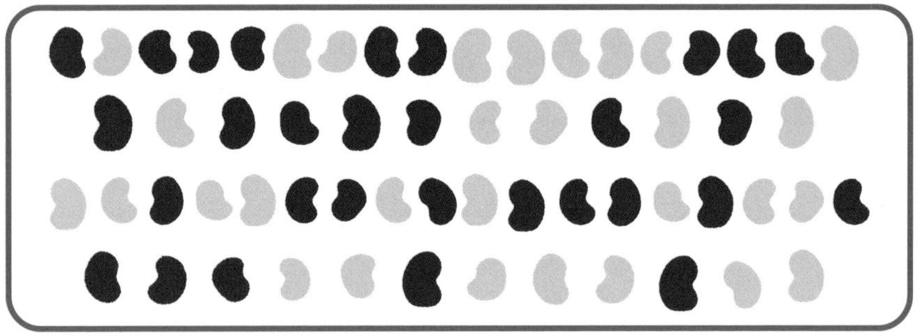

______

10

20

30

40

50

60

Look. Find. Circle. Say.

At home Look in your kitchen. Find sweet, sour, and salty foods.

Review

Look. Draw. Say.

6 *Would you like some (pineapple)? Yes, please. / No, thank you.*

Point. Say. Draw.

I have (cereal / fruit / meat / rice / vegetables / beans) for (breakfast / lunch / dinner).

Look. Find. Match. Say.

Count. Match. Trace. Say.

40

50

60

7 Animals

57 Listen again. Look. Stick. Point.

Look. Match. Say.

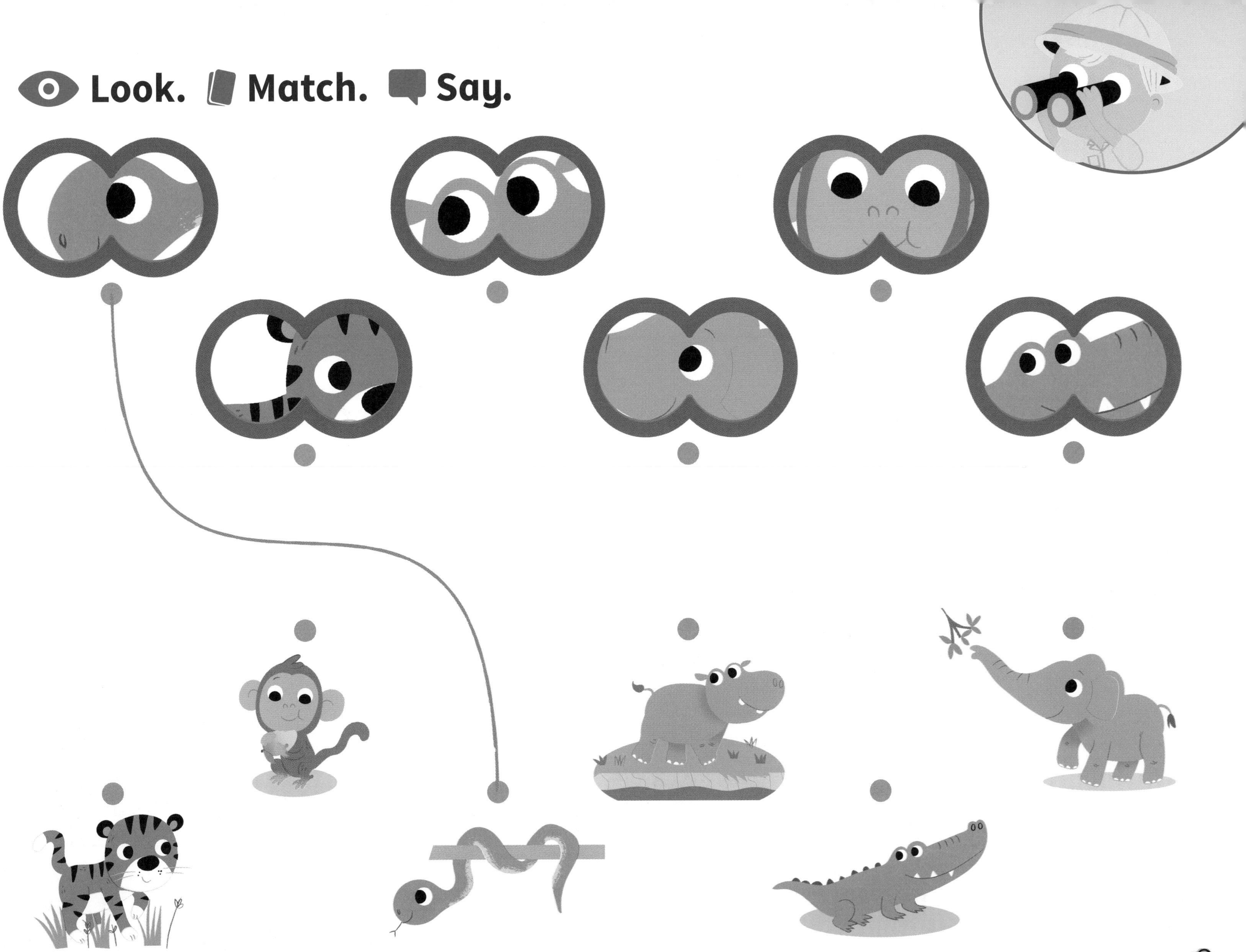

Look. Count. Write. Say.

1

At home

Look in your story books. Find a crocodile, an elephant a monkey, and a snake.

7 **Language practice:** *There's a (monkey). There are (five) (snakes / hippos / tigers / crocodiles). There are lots of (elephants).*

60 **Listen again. Color. Trace. Say.**

3

th

13

20

Listen again. Look. Number.

(61)

Look. Trace.

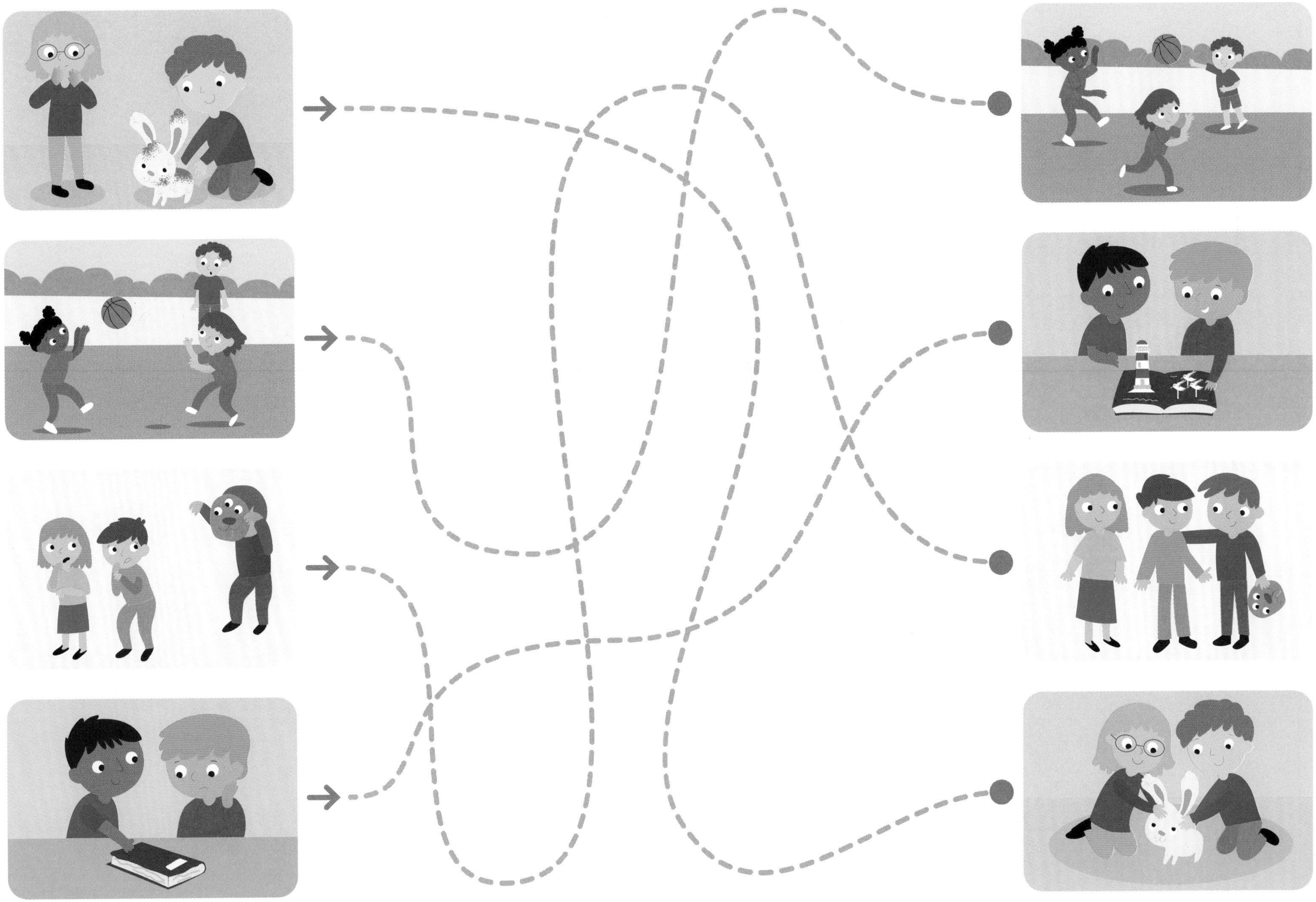

At home When are you friendly?

Look. Find. Circle. Say.

7 **Vocabulary practice:** *giraffes, zebras, ducks, lizards, spiders, parrots*

At home Talk to a friend. Ask *Do you like giraffes? Do you like ducks?*

Look. Find. Circle. Say.

Language practice: *They're (hippos / crocodiles / parrots / giraffes / zebras / lizards). They have (big heads / sharp teeth / long tails / long necks / stripes / short legs).*

Look. Count. Circle. Say.

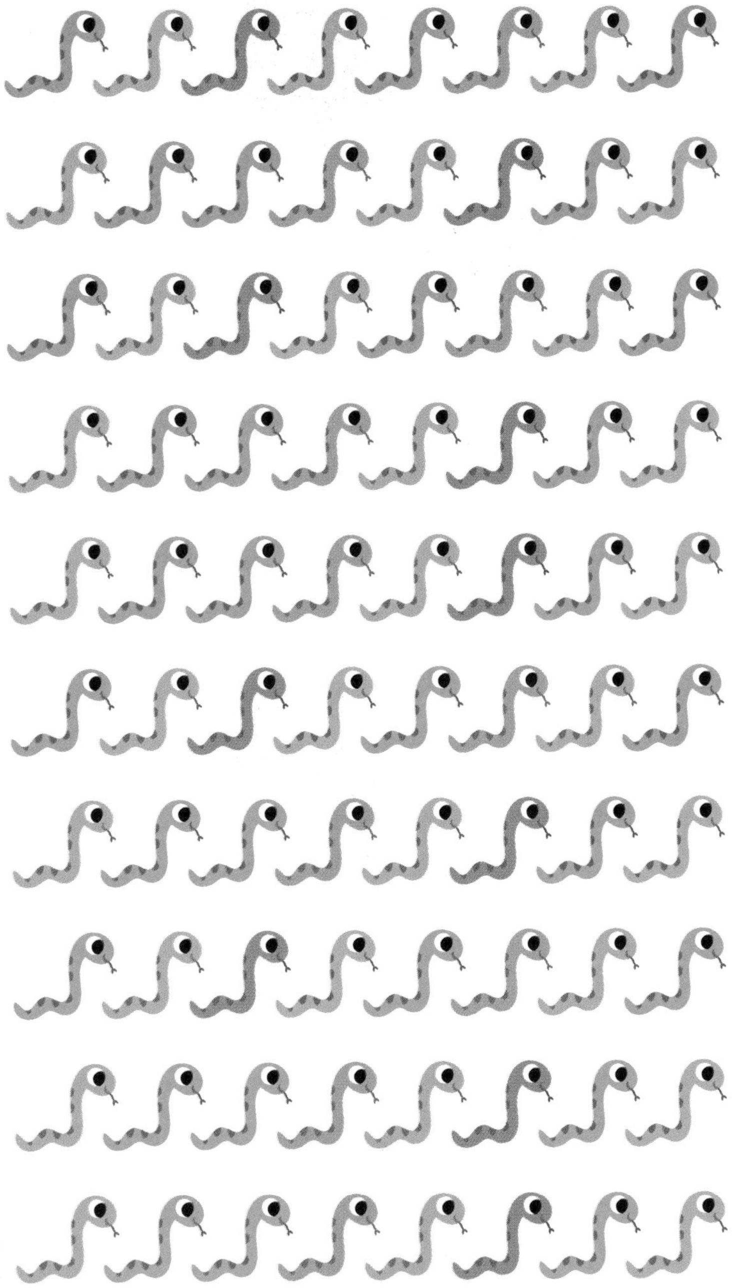

10

20

30

40

50

60

70

80

10

20

30

40

50

60

70

80

Look. Find. Circle. Say.

land

land and water

water

Look. Draw. Say.

They're lizards.
They have long tails.

7 *They're (lizards). They have (long tails) and (short legs).*

Point. Say. Draw.

There's a (crocodile / tiger / hippo). There are (four) (monkeys). There are lots of (snakes / elephants).

8 Plants

67 Listen again. Look. Stick. Point.

Look. Match. Say.

At home Look outside. What can you see?

Look. Circle. Say.

8 **Language practice:** *Plants need (sun / rain / soil).*

70 **Listen again. Find. Circle. Trace. Say.**

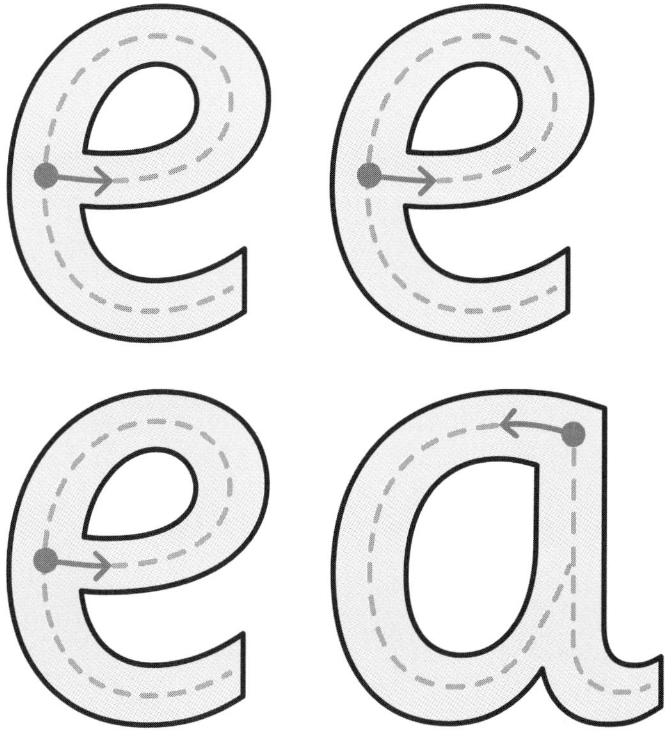

71 Listen again. Look. 123 Number.

Look. Find. Color.

At home

When do you work together?

Look. Find. Circle. Say.

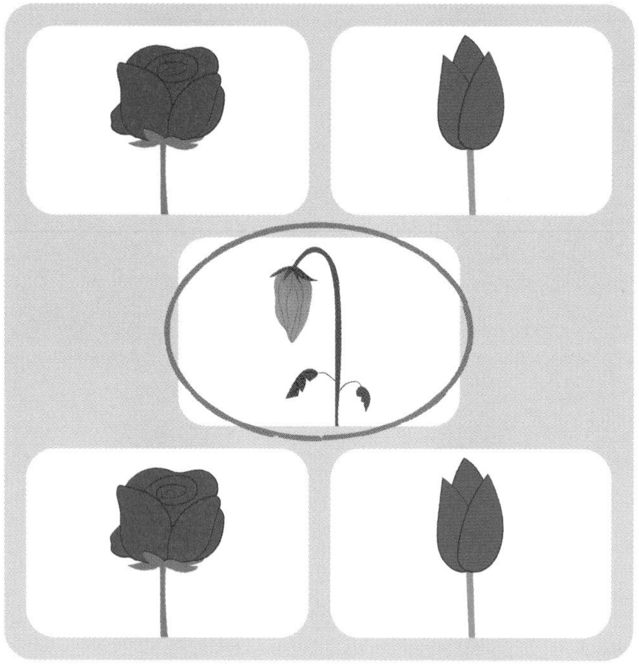

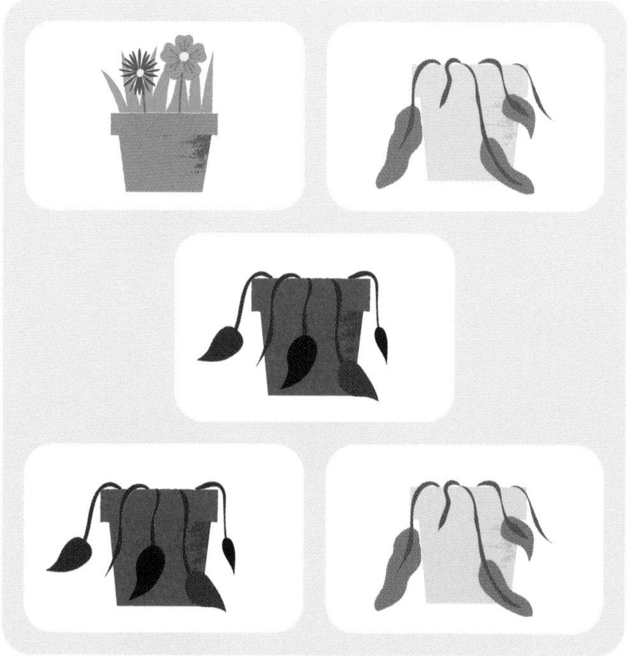

Look. Find. Circle. Say.

Look. Count. Match. Say.

1

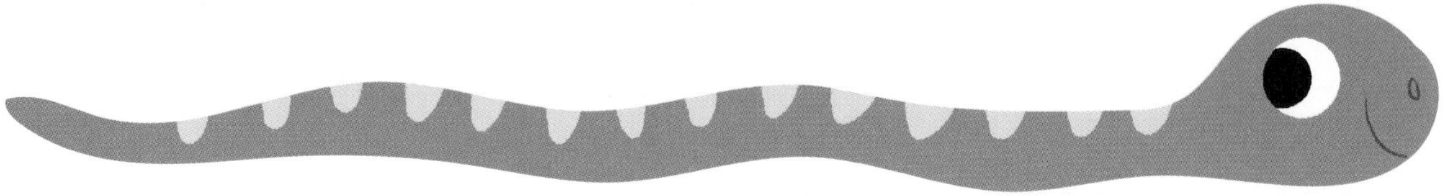

2

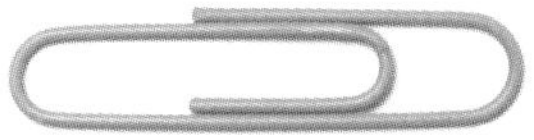

3

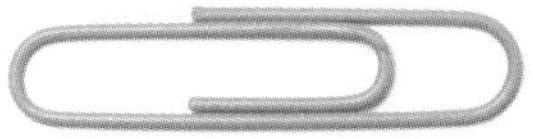

4

5

At home Measure three things with a paperclip.

Look. Match. Say.

1 2 3 4 5 6

Look. Draw. Say.

8 *What (beautiful) (flowers)! What (an old) (tree)!*

Point. Say. Draw.

9 My town

75 Listen again. Look. Stick. Point.

Look. Match. Say.

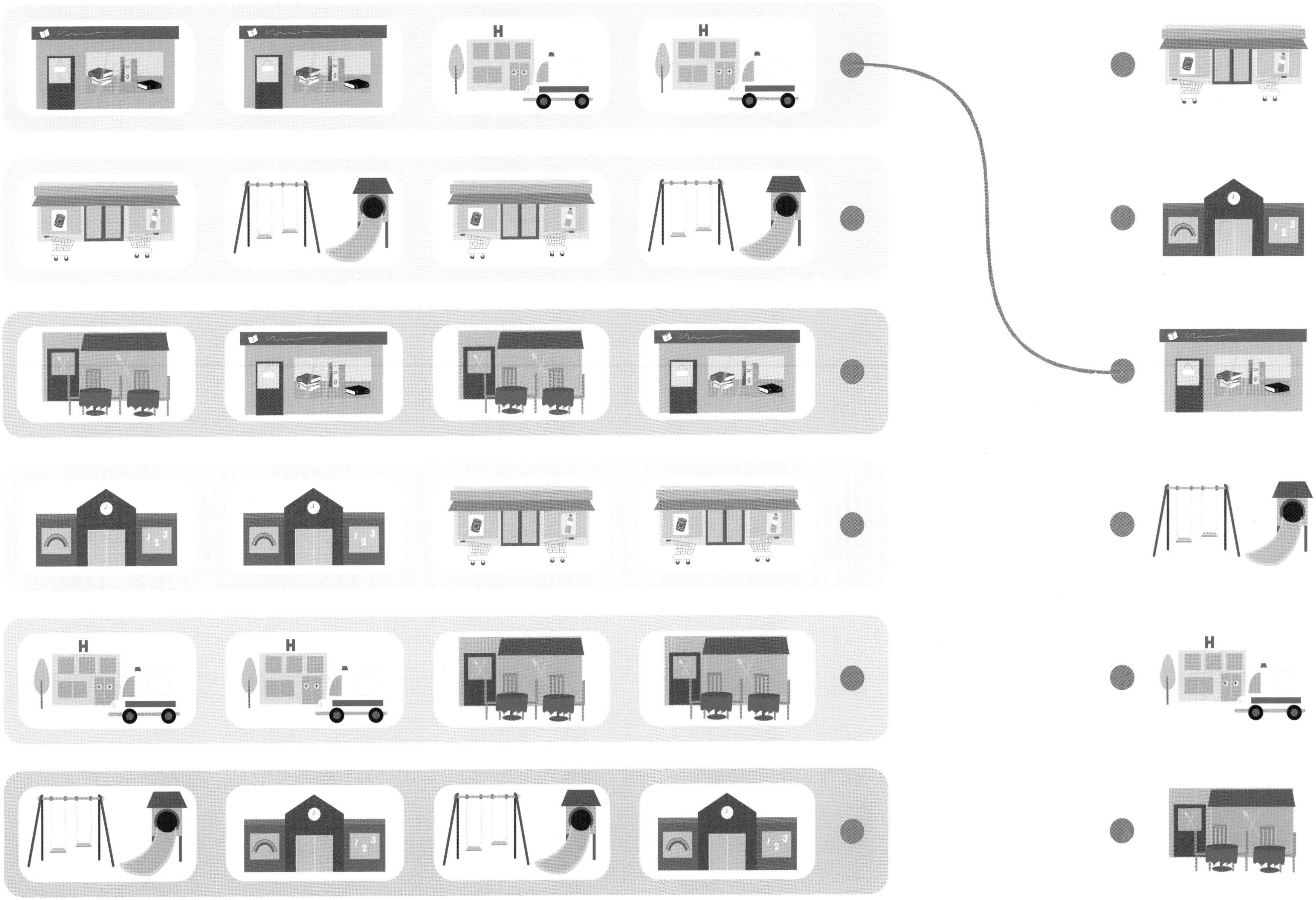

At home What can you see in your town?

Look. Trace. Say.

9 **Language practice:** *Where are you / are we going? I'm / We're going to the (supermarket / hospital / store / school / restaurant / playground).*

78 Listen again. Color. Trace. Say.

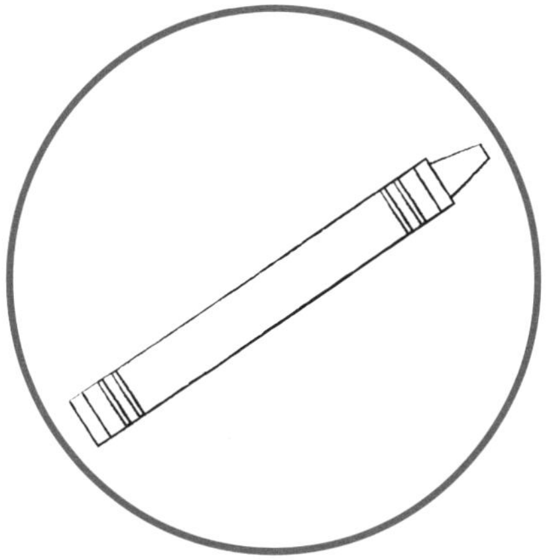

ay ai

Look. Point. Circle.

Look. Trace.

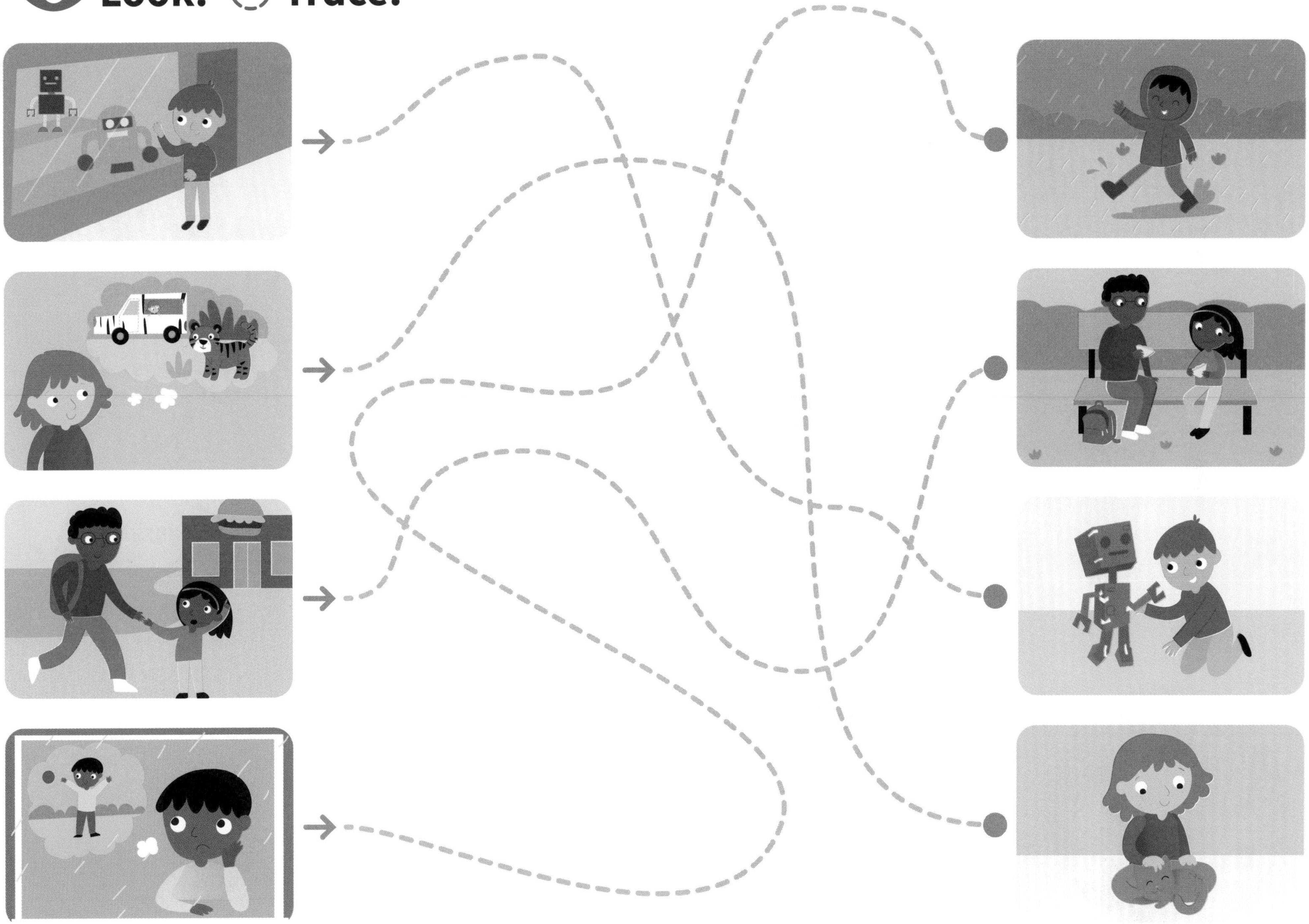

At home What do you appreciate having?

Look. Match. Say.

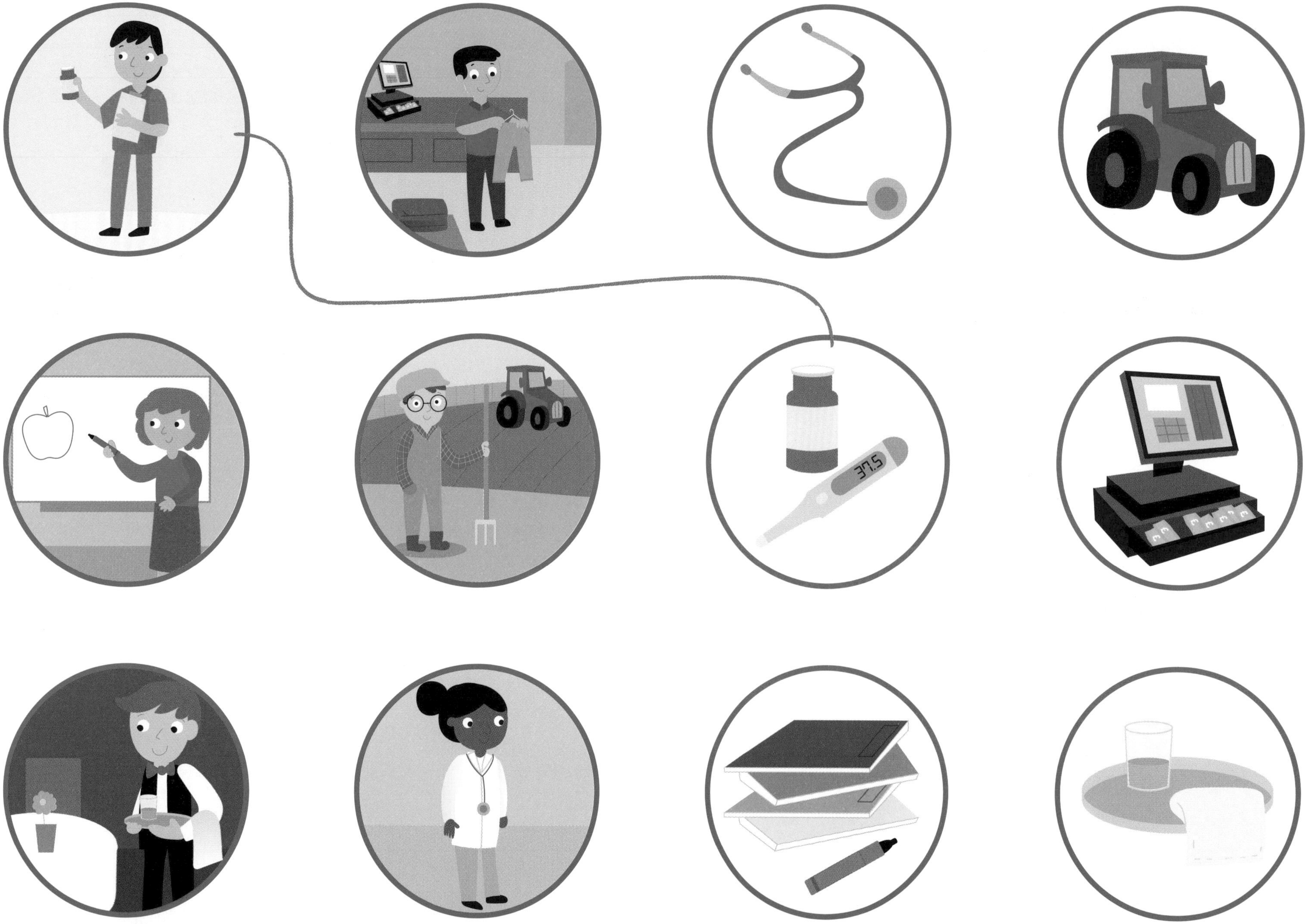

Look. Circle. Say.

Language practice: *teacher, doctor, nurse, waiter, sales clerk, farmer; A (teacher) works (in) a (school). Does a (nurse) work (in) a (hospital)? Yes, (he) does. No, (he) doesn't.*

Look. Count. Circle. Say.

10 20 30 40 50

60 70 80 90 100

10 20 30 40 50

60 70 80 90 100

At home How many fingers does your family have? Count.

Look. Find. Circle. Say.

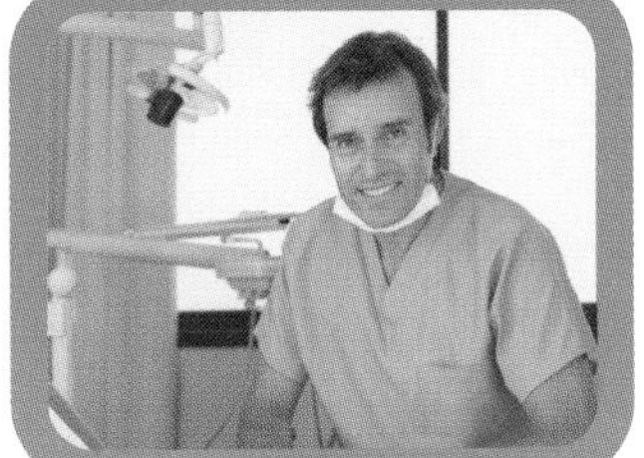

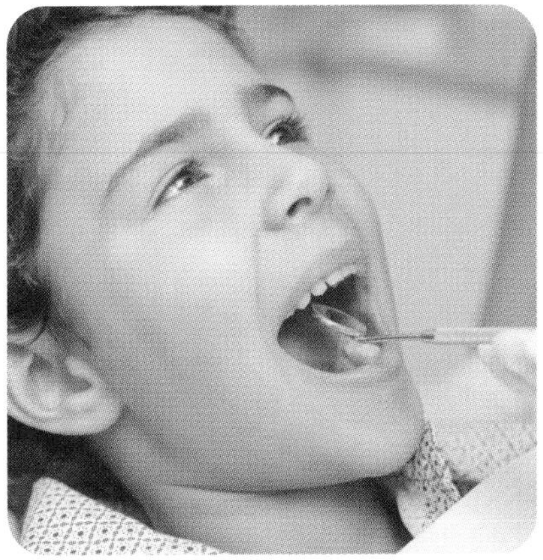
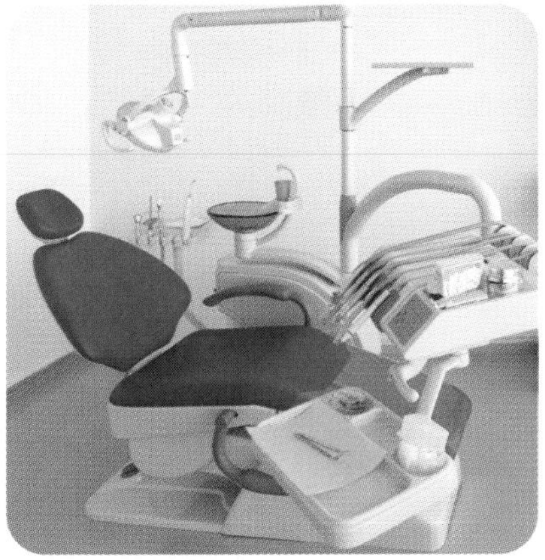

Look. Draw. Say.

I'm going to the store.

Point. Say. Draw.

A sales clerk works in a store.

A (sales clerk / nurse / waiter / teacher / doctor) works (in) a (hospital). A (farmer) works (on) a (farm).

Look. Find. Match. Say.

Count. Match. Trace. Say.

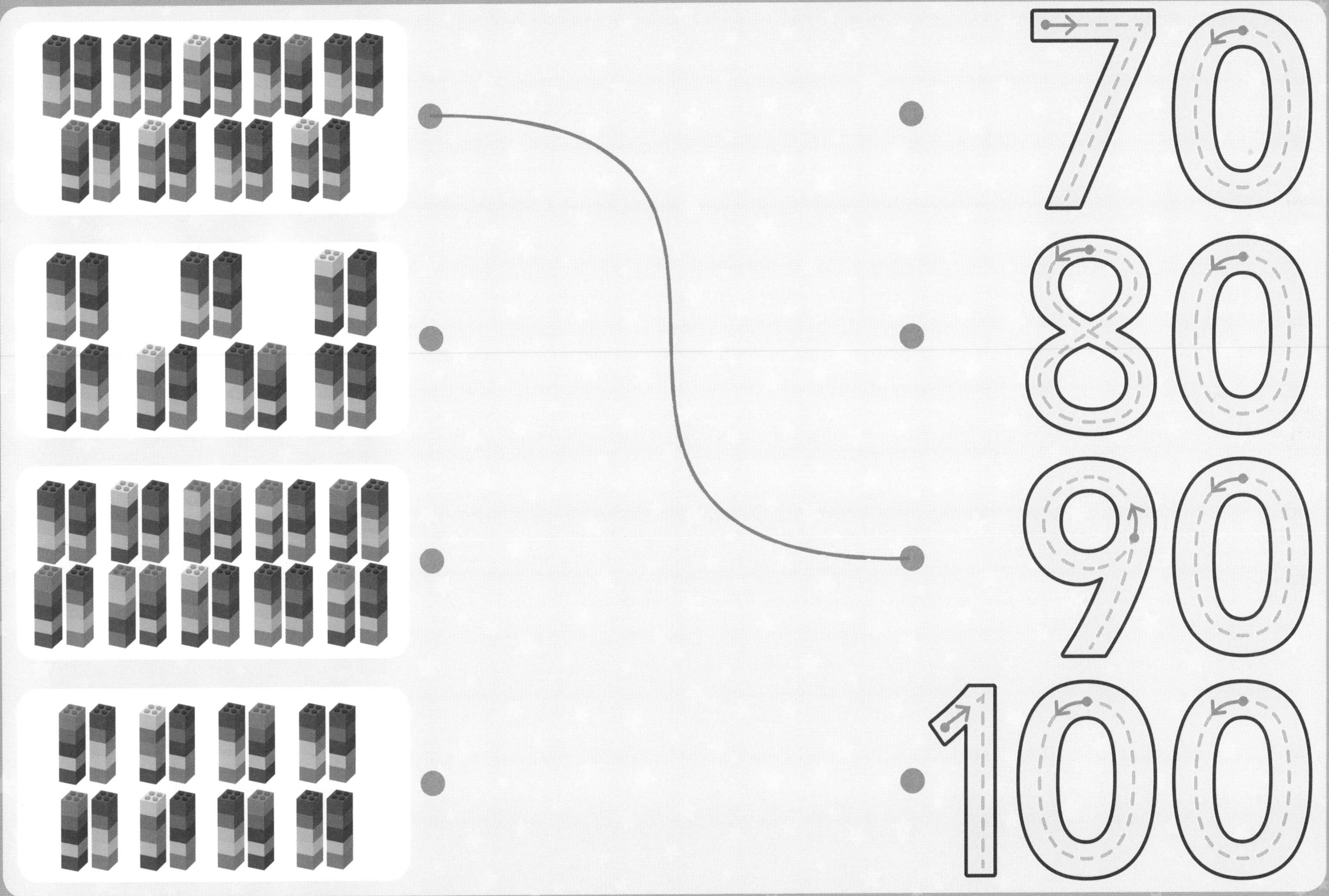

Thanks and Acknowledgements

The publishers and authors would like to thank the following contributors:
Book design and page make-up by Blooberry Design.
Cover design by Blooberry Design.
In-house editing by Zara Hutchinson-Goncalves.
Freelance editing by Catherine Ball, Karen Cleveland Marwick, and Stephanie Howard.
Editorial project management by Emma Ramírez.
Audio recording and production by Leon Chambers.
Original songs and chants by Robert Lee.
Songs and chants production by Jake Carter.

The authors and publishers acknowledge the following sources of copyright material and are grateful for the permissions granted. While every effort has been made, it has not always been possible to identify the sources of all the material used, or to trace all copyright holders. If any omissions are brought to our notice, we will be happy to include the appropriate acknowledgements on reprinting and in the next update to the digital edition, as applicable.

Key: U = Unit.

Photography

All photos are sourced from Getty Images.
U1:imagenavi; **U2:** aldomurillo/E+; David De Lossy/DigitalVision; PeopleImages/iStock/Getty Images Plus; BananaStock; Wavebreakmedia/iStock/Getty Images Plus; Nick David/Photodisc; **U3:** Johannes Mann/The Image Bank; Imgorthand/E+; PhotoAlto/Antoine Arraou; scibak/E+; Lawrence Manning/Corbis; -slav-/iStock/Getty Images Plus; MediaProduction/E+; kertlis/iStock/Getty Images Plus; Sollina Images; jodiejohnson/iStock/Getty Images Plus; John Keeble/Moment; Image Source/DigitalVision; tiler84/iStock / Getty Images Plus; pagadesign/iStock / Getty Images Plus; SKrow/E+; **U5:** katleho Seisa/E+; Kemal Can Habip/EyeEm; Image Source; ajr_images/iStock/Getty Images Plus; Tuul & Bruno Morandi/The Image Bank; Stefan Cristian Cioata/Moment; David Blaikie/Moment; Witthaya Prasongsin/Moment; Nongkran_ch/iStock/Getty Images Plus; Liliya Kulianionak/iStock/Getty Images Plus; Alexander Friedrich/500px; Ronnie Kaufman/DigitalVision; Simon Eeman/EyeEm; **U6:** Sally Anscombe/Stone; Tim UR/iStock/Getty Images Plus; Veeravong Komalamena/EyeEm; vmenshov/iStock/Getty Images Plus; Pineapple Studio/iStock/Getty Images Plus; baibaz/iStock/Getty Images Plus; Kristin Duvall/The Image Bank; OKRAD/iStock/Getty Images Plus; RedHelga/iStock/Getty Images Plus; chonessiStock/Getty Images Plus; **U7:** Maria Spann/Photographer's Choice RF; Magnus Larsson/iStock/Getty Images Plus; isoft/E+; BarbAnna/Moment; Reinhard Dirscherl/The Image bank; Richard A. Whittaker/Moment; Giampaolo Cianella/Moment; Manoj Shah/Stone; GlobalP/iStock/Getty Images Plus; Edmund Lowe Photography/Moment; fenkieandreas/iStock/Getty Images Plus; Andreas Speich/EyeEm; Cristian H. Gomez/EyeEm; **U8:** Kris Wong. www.kriswong.com/Moment; tortoon/iStock/Getty Images Plus; Sarah Palmer/Moment; Lindeblad, Matilda; Nora Carol Photography/Moment; Johner Images; valentinrussanov/E+; Jetta Productions Inc.; DigitalVision; cocorattanakorn/iStock/Getty Images Plus; Steve Hamilton/Photolibrary; DigiPub/Moment; Ashley Jouhar/Photographer's Choice RF; FreshSplash/E+; Guido Mieth/DigitalVision; **U9:** andresr/E+; gerenme/iStock/Getty Images Plus; brankokosteski/iStock/Getty Images Plus; vm/E+; Sam Edwards/OJO Images; Robert Daly/OJO Images; Sitade/iStock/Getty Images Plus; Mint Images; Monty Rakusen/Cultura; artisteer/iStock/Getty Images Plus; Image Source; georgeclerk/iStock/Getty Images Plus; kali9/E+; Jetta Productions Inc./DigitalVision; mokee81/iStock/Getty Images Plus.
Cover photography by NYS444/iStock/Getty Images

Illustrations
Amy Zhing; Beatriz Castro; Begoña Corbalán; Dean Gray; Isabel Nicolle; Louise Forshaw and Collaborate artists; Noopur Thakur.
Cover illustration by Collaborate Agency.